TOMBSTONE HUMOUR

TOMBSTONE HUMOUR

RICHARD DE'ATH

introduced by

SPIKE MILLIGAN.

CHANCELLOR PRESS

Tombstone Humour first published in 1983 by Unwin Paperbacks

Last Will & Testament first published in 1984 by Unwin Paperbacks

Died Laughing first published in 1985 by Unwin Paperbacks

Grave Moments first published in 1986 by Unwin Paperbacks

This collection first published in 1993 by Chancellor Press,
an imprint of Reed International Books Ltd,
Michelin House, 81 Fulham Road, London SW3 6RB

ISBN 1 851 52263 8

Printed in Great Britain by William Clowes, Beccles

CONTENTS

PREFACE

When your name is an ever-present reminder of your ultimate fate, you can perhaps be excused for taking your pleasures seriously. Reading ghost stories, collecting old wills and visiting cemeteries are mine.

Maybe it's inherited (my forebears, all Scots, were a gloomy bunch by all accounts), or else an uncertain childhood (spent under staircases or in air-raid shelters while doodle-bugs screamed overhead during the Second World War), but I happen to be happiest when I'm indulging myself in the macabre side of life – and death. Which is how this book came about.

Because, you see, my predilection for turning up stones to see what dark secrets (figuratively speaking, that is) lie underneath, has given me an enduring fascination with where the dead lie – and, more particularly, *how* the dead lie.

I can remember the moment of revelation as if it were yesterday.

I was a youngster at the time and already had something of a morbid disposition that my relatives thought beyond my years. It was one bright, hot summer day and I had been left to my own devices. Others might have thought a walk across the fields a possible diversion, or a visit to the swimming pool, even the local park for a game of cricket. *I* just happened to fancy the local cemetery.

It was one of those country graveyards where the headstones look like rows of old people's teeth and fight a losing battle in most quarters with encroaching weeds and brambles. A place where the passing years and insidious lichen have

blighted even the proudest examples of the stonemason's art, not to mention the inscriptions so carefully carved proclaiming the love of family and friends for the deceased below.

No doubt on a dark night in the depths of winter, the cemetery would have made a most suitable setting for a horror movie (not that *that* would have frightened away this little ghoul), but on the summer day in question it seemed to offer other equally intriguing delights. (Like the chance of grave-robbing, I hear the cynic declare, already growing bored with my self-analysis.) No – like a chance to see if there were any of my relatives there.

When you spend a childhood being urged to try to 'grow up to be a fine young man like your Uncle Alec' (cut off in his prime), or told 'you'll never be the person your grandfather was unless you work harder at school', it doesn't always favourably incline you towards such departed paragons. Indeed, it gave me an almost malicious determination to see for myself that whatever they might have been, they were now no better than anyone else. Which I suppose is what really drew me to that graveyard.

Anyway, I wandered about for some time among the higgledy-piggledy rows of partly obscured graves – pulling back brambles here, scratching at lichen-covered headstones there – until finally I came across a little clutch of tombs that appeared to be those of my forebears.

There were three inscribed for husbands and their spouses, two for parents (and their children who had apparently squeezed in with them later), and one solitary, small stone with an inscription almost completely worn away by age. I knelt down and cleaned it off with my hands as best I could. Although one or two of the words were still impossible to read, the epitaph was quite unmistakable:

> Here lies Death's wife:
> When this way next you tread,
> Be not surprised should Death himself be dead.

Beneath this were the words: Patience Death, 1784-1838. I chuckled – I just couldn't help it. Not a guffaw or a belly-laugh. Nothing so unseemly. But I did laugh quietly to myself, kneeling there beside the small grave amidst the brambles and weeds.

Who Patience Death was, or what her life had amounted to, I had not the faintest idea. But in that moment she had achieved what is, after all, the whole purpose of an epitaph in a graveyard. She had been remembered. But not sombrely – with a laugh. Unlike most people she was not recalled by flowery words of praise – just an amusing word play on her name.

Although I didn't know it at the time, this book was as good as conceived at that moment. If one person had gone to her last rest marked by a few pungent lines such as those, I

thought, there must have been others. And I thought it would be fun to find them.

So on summer days and winter afternoons since then I have spent many a happy hour wandering where the dead lie – and often prove it by insisting they are merely sleeping. I have also combed many old record books and documents for examples of gravestone wit and humour that, like the people they commemorate, have long since mouldered into dust.

All the epitaphs I have found fall into one of four categories it seems. There are the commonplace unobjectionable ones (name, dates and a line or two of pious text on the worthy buried therein), and the commonplace objectionable ('Affliction sore from her, Long time I bore'). Then there are the intentionally grotesque epitaphs (like that on the barrister Sir John Strange, 'Here lies an honest lawyer – That is Strange.'), and the grotesque unintentional ('Here lies the corpse of Dr Chard – Who filled up half of this churchyard.').

The first category is vast: the other three less so, naturally, but still to be found about our cemeteries as the following pages, in which they are gathered together in various groups, will amply demonstrate. Obviously, no guarantee on the authenticity of every one is given, though the locations have been checked as carefully as possible. Some of them, as you will read, no one in their right mind – or even out of it – would want to be caught dead with!

So thanks to those many folk who helped in the compiling of this book, clergymen, church-wardens, cemetery keepers, grave-diggers (and even some cheerful Australians) – and in particular the late Patience Death and the very present Spike Milligan. Let me leave you with my favourite lines of graveyard humour: not from a tombstone but from the pen of James Thurber.

'Nat Bruge', wrote the great humorist, 'watched the moon coming up lazily out of the old cemetery in which nine of his daughters were lying. And only two of them were dead.'

Richard De'Ath
July 1982

INTRODUCTION
by Spike Milligan

Since time began, man has held death in various states of emotional and intellectual dilemma and awe. What was it, an end or a beginning? The most positive thing he's done, is to disdain it: i.e. great acts of heroism in the face of danger. Even to this day, the greatest and most revered awards are ones for heroism – in America, the Congressional Medal of Honour, and our own, older, Victoria Cross. But in many philosophies (and my own) the answer is laughter, but this has only been a comparatively recent innovation in man's approach to death. Roundabout AD 1500 mildly humorous remarks started to appear on tombstones:

> Here lyes Margaret Young
> Who had sheed lived
> Would surely been hung
> By the length of her tongue.

Now this was a daring innovation when you consider the awe of say *Australopithecus* – who reverently bound the deceased in the sitting position, smeared the corpse with red clay, hoping that the colour and position of the body might deceive the Doppelganger into believing the corpse to be still alive – or the incredible finery of the dead Pharaohs. The thought of a comic comment on the pyramids would have been greeted with horror, even death.

But, as I say, since 1500(ish) there has been a genuine progress in cutting back the 'Reaper's' grisly image by a change of emphasis, until, in 1800, you get genuine comic gems like this:

> Here lies the body
> of Mabel Charlotte
> Born a virgin
> Died a harlot
> She was a virgin
> Till her 21st year
> A remarkable thing
> In Oxfordshire.

It shows a psychological courage as against the obvious physical one; for the hero who beat death, the danger was over – but not for the village joker who, on the following epitaph:

> Pray you all
> For the Vicar's daughter
> Millicent Ann
> Who died as pure
> As the day she began

then added,

> Not afore, in this village,
> She had every man.

He must have looked over his shoulder of a dark night for many a year!

I myself have never desecrated a tombstone, not even in fun, but I had cause to concoct an epitaph. During the war in

North Africa I befriended a wild dog – we called him Havelock Ellis. No one was sadder than I when he was shot in the head one dark night when he attacked a sentry, so I wrote:

> Here lies the body
> of Havelock the dog
> Shot thru the head
> And dropped like a log
> If he'd have been smart
> And not bit Gunner Fred
> This little dog
> Would not be dead.

I was heartbroken at his death – and yet it seemed better he had a funny epitaph when he died.

Man will forever be battling against death – sometimes with horrific results. I have seen old people who were no more than slow pulsating vegetables – they wanted to go, if they were told they were going to be put to sleep they would have been *happy*. There is a time to live, a time to die, a time to laugh, and at no time are the three of them very far apart.

I myself have my epitaph. It will read:

> 'I demand a Second Opinion.'

Read this book, which has obviously been put together with love and gales of laughter, and buy a few for your friends, the

older the better. Why not lie down in the garden with this book and a shovel, and make up your own epitaph? Better still, make up one about someone you hate, like the Inland Revenue:

> The man who ruined me for life
> Was this damn Tax Inspector
> But he tripped and fell upon a knife
> And now he's just a spectre.

And, remember, you'll never get to heaven alive!

19

TOMBSTONE
HUMOUR

or
The Coffin They Carried Them
Off In!

CRUEL FATE

First a Cough
Carried Me Off
Then a Coffin
They Carried Me Off In!
From a disappeared headstone in Boston, America

Poor Martha Snell! Her's gone away.
Here would if her could, but her couldn't stay.
Her'd two sore legs, and a badish cough,
But her legs it was as carried her off.

On a tomb in Staverton churchyard,
Gloucestershire

Here lies Jane Hitchen, who when her glass was spent,
Kicked up her heels – and away she went!

In Bury St Edmunds, Suffolk

Here lieth the body of Betty Cowden,
Who would live longer but she couden,
Sorrow and grief made her decay,
Till her bad leg carried her away.

On a memorial stone in Hitchin, Hertfordshire

Here lies John Bunn,
Who was killed by a gun,
His name wasn't Bunn, but his real name was Wood,
But Wood wouldn't rhyme with gun,
  so I thought Bunn should.

From a gravestone in Southampton, Hampshire

Sacred to the memory of
MAJOR JAMES BRUSH, Royal Artillery
who was killed by the accidental discharge
of a pistol by his orderly, 14th April, 1831
Well done, good and faithful servant.

In Woolwich churchyard, London

Erected to the memory of
JOHN PHILLIPS
Accidentally Shot
As a mark of affection by his brother.

On a gravestone in Ulster

Erected to the memory of
JOHN MACFARLANE
Drowned in the Water of Leith
By a few affectionate friends.

Leith churchyard, Lothian

Against his will
Here lies George Hill.
Who from a cliff
Fell down quite stiff.
When it happened is not known,
Therefore not mentioned on this tomb.

In St Peter's churchyard, Isle of Thanet

A ponderous load on me did fall,
And killed me dead against this wall.

On a tomb in Dean churchyard, Bolton,
Lancashire

In memory of the Clerk's son:
Bless my i
Here I lies,
In a sad pickle
Killed by an icicle.

From a grave in Bampton Parish
Church, Devon

Here lie the bones of Lazy Fred,
Who wasted precious time in bed.
Some plaster fell down on his head,
And thanks be praised – our Freddie's dead.

On the tomb of Frederick Twitchell in
Leeds, Yorkshire

Here lies Tommy Montague
Whose love for angling daily grew;
He died regretted, while late out,
To make a capture of a trout.

In Sutton Mallet cemetery, Somerset

Here lies poor but honest Bryan Tunstall,
He was a most expert angler,
Until Death, envious of his mark,
Threw out his line, hooked him and landed him here.

From Whitby cemetery, Yorkshire

These vales were saddened by no
  common gloom
When good Jemima perished in her bloom.
When, such the awful will of Heaven, she died
By flames breathed on her from her own fireside.

On Jemima Bridges, who was burned to death in
Rydal, Cumbria

Here lies John Dalyrymple
He picked a pimple.
On a grave in Thrustonville, America

Here lies a man who was killed by lightning;
He died when his prospects seemed to be brightening.
He might have cut a flash in this world of trouble,
But the flash cut him, and he lies in the stubble.
In Great Torrington churchyard, Devon

To all my friends I bid adieu
A more sudden death you never knew.
As I was leading the mare to drink
She kicked and killed me
Quicker'n a wink.
At Melton Mowbray Parish Church, Leicestershire

Fair Maiden Lilliard lies under this stone:
Little was her stature, but great was her fame;
Upon the English lions she had laid many thumps,
And when her legs were cut off, she fought on her
    stumps!

*On Maiden Lilliard who fought with great bravery at
Ancrum Moor, Roxburgh, where she is buried*

One Thomas buried here whose fate was such,
To lose his life by wrestling much
Which may a warning be to all
If they into such Pastimes fall.

*On Thomas Hawkins, who died at 28, in
Mary Tavy, Devon*

Here lies interr'd a man o' micht,
His name was Malcolm Downie;
He lost his life, on market nicht,
By fa'in off his pownie.

On a grave in Cullen graveyard, GrampianOne

Here is Lays
Killed by a chaise.
On the tomb of ostler William Prichard in
Frodsham churchyard, Cheshire

Here interred George Anderson doth lie,
By falling on an anchor he did die.
On a tomb in Minster, Kent

Here lies the body of Andrew Gear,
Whose mouth did stretch from ear to ear;
Stranger, step lightly o'er his head,
For if he gapes, by Josh, you're dead!
From a tomb in a Sunderland cemetery

The Lord saw good, I was lopping off wood,
And down fell from the tree:
I met with a check, and I broke my neck
And so death lopped off me.

On a memorial stone in Ockham, Surrey

Here lies Matthew Hollingshead,
Who died from cold caught in his head.
It brought on fever and rheumatiz,
Which ended me – for here I is.

At Fosbrooke in Northumberland

Constance Bevon, wife of John,
Lies beneath this marble stone;
Fat and buxom, round and stout,
'Twas apoplexy bowled her out.

From a disappeared grave in Cumbria

Here lyeth the body of
SIMON GILKETT
Who was killed by a rockett.

In Milton Regis parish churchyard, Kent

Blown Upward
Out of Sight
He Sought The Leak
By Candlelight

On a headstone in Collingbourne Ducis,
Wiltshire

In Memory of
ELLEN SHANNON
Who was fatally burned by the
explosion of a lamp filled with
Danforth's Non-Explosive Fluid.

In Girard cemetery, Pennsylvania, America

Here lies an honest independent man,
Boast more ye great ones if ye can;
I have been kicked by a bull and ram,
Now let me lay contented as I am.

On the gravestone of James Amies at
Holy Trinity Church, Stalham, Norfolk

Weep, stranger, for a father spilled,
From a stage coach, and thereby killed;
His name was John Sykes, a maker of sassengers,
Slain with three other outside passengers.

In New Jersey, America

Here lies John Adams, who received a thump
Right on the forehead, from the parish pump,
Which gave him the quietus in the end,
Tho' many doctors did his case attend.

On a grave in Wellingborough, Northamptonshire

Here lies entombed one Roger Morton,
Whose sudden death was early brought on!
Trying one day his corns to mow off,
The razor slipped and cut his toe off!
The toe, or rather what it grew to,
An inflammation quickly flew to;
The part then took to mortifying,
And poor dear Roger took to dying.

On a grave in Acton cemetery, Cornwall

Here lies old
Aunt HANNAH PROCTER
Who purged but didn't call the Doctor.
She couldn't stay
She had to go
Praise be to God from whom
All blessings flow.

In Queenborough cemetery, Medway, Kent

She was not smart; she was not fair,
But hearts with grief are swellin'
All empty stands her little chair,
She died of eatin' watermelon.

From Teaneck cemetery, America

In Memory of
THOMAS FROST
Who died of Cholera Morbus
caused by eating green fruit
In the certain hope of a
blessed immortality
Reader, go thou and do likewise.

In Grantham churchyard, Lincolnshire

Here lies Johnny Cole,
Who died, on my soul,
After eating a plentiful dinner;
While chewing his crust,
He was turned into dust,
With his crimes undigested – poor sinner.

*From a disappeared grave in
Melton Mowbray, Leicestershire*

He Got a Fishbone in his Throat
Which made him sing an Angel's note.

On a headstone in Beacon Falls, America

Here I lies with my two daughters,
Killed by drinking Cheltenham Waters;
If we had stuck to Epsom Salts,
We wouldn't be lying in these vaults.

On a headstone in St Giles' Church,
Cheltenham, Gloucestershire

Here lies the body of our Dear Anna,
Done to death by a Banana.
It wasn't the fruit that dealt the blow
But the skin of the thing that laid her low!

In Burlington, America

Eliza, sorrowing
Rears this marble slab
To her dear John
Who died of eating crab.

From Crowton cemetery, Cheshire

By many folks it has been said,
The only staff of life is bread,
How could it then stop Simon's breath,
And be the occasion of his death?
One little morsel proved his last,
Which he devoured in so much haste,
That angry Death in passion swore,
He ne'er should swallow one bit more.

On the tomb of Simon Chambers in
Lowestoft, Suffolk

Here lie the bones of Joseph Jones,
Who ate while he was able;
But, once o'erfed, he dropped down dead,
And fell beneath the table.
When from the tomb, to meet his doom,
He rises amidst sinners;
Since he must dwell, in Heaven or Hell,
Take him – which gives best dinners!

*On a headstone in Wolverhampton
Church, Staffordshire*

Under this stone
Lies a Reverend Drone;
Who preached against sin
With a terrible grin;
In which some may think that he acted but oddly,
Since he lived by the wicked and not by the godly.

From Newgate, London

Here lies cut down like unripe fruit
The wife of DEACON AMOS SHUTE
She died of drinking too much coffee
Anny Dominy 1840.

On a grave in Bedrule Parish Church, Roxburgh

Here lies
RANDOLPH PETER
Of Oriel, the Eater,
Whoe'er you are, tread softly, I entreat you,
For if he chance to wake, be sure he'll eat you.

From a disappeared grave in Plymouth, Devon

Grim Death took me without any warning,
I was well at night
And dead at nine in the morning!

On a tomb in Sevenoaks churchyard, Kent

Here lies the body of Mary Ann Lowder,
She burst while drinking a Seidlitz Powder:
Called from this world to her Heavenly rest:
She drank it and she effervesced.

In Burlington cemetery, America

Here in this Urn from Malabar
The ashes lie of Jonathan Barr;
He sought a higher life afar
And travelled homeward in a Jar.

From Nantucket graveyard, America

Let the wind go free,
Where'er thou be,
For twas the wind,
That killed me!

In Leyland churchyard, Lancashire

He Called Bill Smith
A Lier.

*On a wooden headboard in
Cripple Creek, America*

Underful this marble fair,
Lies the body entombed of Gervase Aire;
He died not of an ague fit,
Nor surfeited by too much wit
Methinks this was a wondrous death
That **Aire** should die for want of breath.

On a gravestone in St Giles' Church,
Cripplegate, London

Hallowed be the Sabbath,
And farewell all worldly Self;
The Week begins on Tuesday,
For Munday hath hanged himself.

On the grave of James Munday in
Fulham, London.

Here lies the body of P. M. Haskell,
He lived a knave and died a rascal.

From a disappeared grave in
Islington, London

Here lies the swift racer, so famed for his running,
In spite of his boasting, his swiftness, and cunning;
In leaping o'er ditches, and skipping o'er fields,
Death soon overtook him, and tript up his heels.

From the tomb of a noted runner in
St John's Church, Chester

Judge, reader, what he did lose
Who lost but breath
Lived to die well,
And died a **Meredeth**.

On church organist, Thomas Meredeth, at
Marsfield, Somerset

OWEN MOORE
Gone away
Ow'n more
Than he could pay.

In St John's Church, Battersea, London

Mary had a little waist,
She laced it smaller still;
A stone o'er Mary has been placed
Out on the silent hill.
And on that stone these words are writ,
'Oh, let us hope she's gone,
Where angels never care 'it,
'Bout what they have got on!'

*Epitaph on the dangers of lacing a corset
too tight. In the West Riding of Yorkshire*

Here lies Sir John Hawkins,
Without his shoes or his stawkings.

*On the Manchester grave of the author of
'History of Music'*

Beneath this stone a lump of clay,
Lies Uncle PETER DANIELS.
Too early in the month of May,
He took off his Winter flannels.

In Chatham cemetery, Kent

Here lies a lewd fellow,
Who while he drew breath,
In the midst of life,
Was in quest of death.
Which he quickly obtained
For it cost him his life,
For being in bed
With another man's wife.

From a disappeared grave in Bath

Here lies poor Charlotte,
Who died no Harlot;
But in her Virginity,
At the age of Nineteen,
In this vicinity
Is rarely to be found or seen.

On a headstone in Cardiff cemetery

Here lies
HERMINA KUNTZ
To Virtue Quite Unknown.
Jesus Rejoice!
At Last She Sleeps Alone.

At Belle Isle, America

In this here grave ye see before ye
Lies buried up a dismal story
A young maiden crossed in love
And taken to the realms above.
But he that crossed her, I should say,
Deserves to go the other way!

In Pentewan graveyard, Cornwall

Little Willy in the best of sashes,
Played with fire and was burnt to ashes!
Very soon the room got chilly,
But no one liked to poke poor Willy!

From a cemetery in Montana, America

This little hero that lies here,
Was conquered by the Diarrheer.

On a headstone in Portland cemetery,
Vermont, America

Oped my eyes, took a peep;
Didn't like it, went to sleep.

On an infant's grave in Worcester

Here lie the bodies of three children dear,
Two at Llanwonno and One here.

In Vaynore churchyard, nr. Merthyr Tydfil,
Mid Glamorgan

Here lie the
Jones Boys Twins
As Dead as Nits:
One died of Fever
One of Fits.

> On a grave in Sierra City cemetery,
> America

Two Littleboys lie here,
Yet strange to say
These little boys are girls.

> On the grave of twins, Emma and Maria
> Littleboy, in Hornsey cemetery, London

Death has taken little Jerry,
Son of Joseph and Seran Howells.
Seven days he wrestled with the dysentery
Then he perished in his little bowels.

> In Stow cemetery, Lincolnshire

In Affectionate remembrance of JOSEPH VAIL
Who died September 18th 1875
Aged 16 years
'The Traction Engine Wheel Upon Me Fell
I Had Not Time To Bid My Friends Farewell!'
Welby churchyard, nr. Grantham, Lincolnshire

Beneath this stone our baby lies,
He neither cries nor hollers;
He lived on earth just twenty days,
And cost us forty dollars.
From Burlington, America

God works wonders now and then;
Here lies a lawyer and an honest man.

To which an unknown hand has added:

This is a mere law quibble, not a wonder;
Here lies a lawyer, and his client under.
From a memorial stone in Walworth, London

Within this tomb lies the world's chiefest Rose,
She who was sweet will now offend your nose.

> *On the grave of Rosamond Clifford, mistress to*
> *Henry II, at Godstow, Oxford*

Here I lie at the Chapel door,
Here lie I because I'm poor,
The farther in the more you'll pay,
Here lie I as warm as they.

> *On the tomb of Robert Phillip (commonly*
> *called 'Bone' on account of being the chief*
> *parish grave-digger) at the Priest's Door,*
> *Kingsbridge Church, Devon*

Here lies the Hope of a fond Mother
And the Blasted expectations of a disappointed Father.
The wedding day appointed was
And wedding clothes provided,
But ere that day did come, alas!
He sickened and he die did.

> *On a tomb in Bideford churchyard, Devon*

Six feet beneath
This funeral wreath
Is laid upon the shelf
One Jerry Jones,
Who dealt in bones,
And now he's bones himself.

On a tomb nr. Taunton, Somerset

Underneath this sod lies JOHN ROUND
Who was lost in the sea, and never was found.

At Watton churchyard, Norfolk

Here lies JOHN HIGLEY
Whose father and mother were drowned on their passage
from America.
Had both lived, they would be buried here.

In Belturbet churchyard, Ireland

Stranger, pause and shed a tear,
For May Jane lies buried here,
Mingled in a most surprising manner,
With Susan, Joy and portions of Hannah!
On a memorial plaque noting the reburial of the ashes of four
wives spilled from their urns during a storm.
In Ringwood churchyard, Kent

GRAVE THOUGHTS

Remember me as you pass by
As you are now, so once was I,
As I am now, you soon will be,
Therefore prepare to follow me.

To which was later added:

To follow you I'm not content
Until I know which way you went.
On a grave in Great Burstead Church, Essex

Life is a jest, and all things show it;
I thought so once, now I know it.
On the tomb of the poet John Gay
in Westminster Abbey

Man's life is but a winter's day
Some only breakfast and away
Others to dinner stay and are full fed
The oldest man but sups and goes to bed
Long is his life who lingers out the day
Who goes the soonest has the least to pay.

On a headstone in Bamwell Priory Church,
Northamptonshire

Gentle Reader,
Look on the spot where I do lie;
I was always a very good feeder,
But now the worms do feed on I.

At St Paul's Church, Bedford

Here lies father, and mother, and sister, and I.
We all died within the space of one year.
They all be buried at Whimble, except I,
And I be buried here.

At Edworth, Bedfordshire

Where I am gone, you are coming;
So be serious, stop your funning.
From a grave in Winstone churchyard, Yorkshire

Here lies my corpse, who was the man
That loved a sop in the dripping pan;
But now, believe me, I am dead,
See how the pan stands at my head.
Still for the sops till the last I cried,
But could not eat, and so I died.
My neighbours, they perhaps will laugh
When they do read my epitaph.
On a grave in Woodditton, Cambridgeshire

As you are in health and spirits gay,
I was, too, the other day;
I thought myself of life as safe
As those that read my epitaph.
In Byfield Church, Northamptonshire

Here I lie and no wonder I'm dead,
For the wheel of the waggon went over my head.

On a grave in Prendergast churchyard, Dyfed

From earth my body first arose
But here to earth again it goes,
I never desire to have it more
To plague me as it did before.

From a monument in Llangurig churchyard,
Powys

He lived and died a true Christian,
He loved his friends, and hated his enemies.

In Dundee, Tayside

The horse bit the parson,
How came that to pass?
The horse heard the parson say,
All flesh is grass!

On Reverend Michael Jones' tomb
at Welwyn, Hertfordshire

'All flesh is grass'
The Scriptures they do say,
And grass when dead
Is turned into hay.
Now when the reapers her away do take
My, what a whopping haystack she will make!

From the headstone of an exceedingly
fat woman in Kersey, Suffolk

Born in America, in Europe bred,
In Africa travell'd and in Asia dead.

On a grave in Wrexham Church, Clwyd

If your nose is close to the grindstone
And you hold it there long enough
In time you'll say there's no such thing
As brooks that babble and birds that sing
These three will all your world compose –
Just you, the stone and your poor old nose.

From a disappeared gravestone in Enfield,

Greater London

Our bodies are like shoes, which off we cast;
Physic their cobblers, and death their last.
In Cirencester churchyard, Gloucestershire

Here lies my guid an' gracious Aunty,
Whom Death has packed in his portmanty.
From a tombstone in Ross and Cromarty graveyard,
Scotland

I am here, I am there, do you know where?
When I was alive, 'twas that made me stare.
In Old St Pancras cemetery, London

Now I am dead and laid in my grave
And that my bones are rotten,
By this shall I remembered be,
Or else I am forgotten.
On a grave in Uckfield, East Sussex

Whoever here on Sunday,
Will practise playing at ball,
It may be before Monday,
The Devil will have you all!

On a stone in the graveyard in Llanvair
Discoed, Gwent

Pain was my portion,
Physic was my food;
Groans my devotion
Drugs did me no good.

From Oldbury-on-Severn Church,
Gloucestershire

Here lies one who for medicines would not give
A little gold, and so his life he lost;
I fancy now he'd wish again to live,
Could he but guess how much his funeral cost.

In Sheffield cemetery, Yorkshire

SHALL WEE ALL DIE?
WEE SHALL DIE ALL.
ALL DIE SHALL WEE?
DIE ALL WEE SHALL.

On an unusual grave in Cunwallow,
nr. Helston, Cornwall

An honest fellow here is laid,
His debts in full he always paid;
And, what's more strange, the neighbours tell us,
He always brought back borrowed umbrellas.

From a tomb in Los Angeles, California, America

Underneath this ancient mill
Lies the body of poor Will;
Odd he lived and odd he died,
And at his funeral nobody cried;
Where he's gone and how he fares,
Nobody knows, and nobody cares.

In Canterbury cemetery, Kent

We must all die, there is no doubt;
Your glass is running – mine is out.

On a monument in Shoreditch
churchyard, London

If there is a future world
My lot will not be bliss;
But if there is no other
I've made the most of this.

From Desingwoke cemetery, America

Praises on tombs are trifles vainly spent,
A man's good name is his best monument.

In Carmarthen churchyard, Dyfed

Friend, in your epitaphs I'm grieved
So very much is said.
One half will never be believed,
The others never read.
   On an epitaph writer buried in Chiswick, London

Reader, pass on, nor waste your precious time
On bad biography and murdered rhyme:
What I was before's well known to my neighbours
What I am now is no concern of yours.
   On the grave of William Ash at West Down, Devon

HOLY DEADLOCK

Here lies the body of
JAMES ROBINSON
and RUTH, his wife.
'Lord, their warfare is accomplished'.

On a grave in St Saviour's Church,
Hackney, London

Here lies my poor wife, without bed or blanket,
But dead as a door nail. God by thankit.

In Bradford cemetery, Yorkshire

Here lies my poor wife,
A sad slatern and shrew,
If I said I regretted her
I should lie too.

On a headstone in Texas, America

Here is my much loved Celia laid,
At rest from all her earthly labours!
Glory to God! Peace to the Dead!
And to the ears of all her neighbours.

On a tomb in Southampton graveyard

Here lies Jemmy Little, a carpenter industrious,
A very good-natured man, but somewhat blusterous.
When that his little wife his authority withstood,
He took a little stick and banged her as he would.
His wife now left alone, her loss does so deplore,
She wishes Jemmy back to bang her a little more;
For now he's dead and gone this fault appears so small,
A little thing would make her think it was no fault at all.

In Portsmouth cemetery, Hampshire

Beneath this stone lies one whose life,
Was spent in quarrels and in strife.
Wake not his spirit from its rest,
For when he slept the world was blest.

On the grave of Michael Collins, Gravesend, Kent

Beneath this stone lies Katherine, my wife,
In death my comfort, and my plague through life.
Oh, liberty! But soft, I must not boast,
She'll haunt me else, by jingo, with her ghost!

On the tomb of Katherine Leary in Belfast

Here lies the mother of children seven,
Three on earth and four in Heaven;
The four in Heaven preferring rather
To die with mother than live with father.

At Godolphin Cross Church, Cornwall

Here rest my Spouse; no pair through life
So equal lived as we did.
Alike we shared perpetual strife,
Nor knew I rest till she did.

On a grave in Cardiff, South Glamorgan

ELIZA ANN

Has gone to rest.
She now reclines on Abraham's breast:
Peace at last for Eliza Ann,
But not for Father Abraham.

In Farmington cemetery, America

Beneath this stone and not above it
Lie the remains of Anna Lovett;
Be pleased, dear reader, not to shove it,
Lest she should come again above it.
For 'twixt you and I, no one does covet
To see again this Anna Lovett.

On a grave in Enfield, Greater London

Here lies my wife in earthly mould,
Who when she lived did nought but scold.
Peace! wake her not for now she's still;
She had, but now I have my will.

In Ellon churchyard, Grampian

Beneath this stone I do entrust,
Are the remnants of her worthy dust:
Farewell awhile, ye silent tomb,
Until your husband calls for room.

On a monument in Hanwell churchyard, London

Here lies a man, who all his mortal life,
Spent mending clocks, but could not mend his wife.
The alarm of his bell was never so shrill,
As was her tongue clacking like a mill.
But now he's gone – of whither none can tell –
I hope beyond the sound of his wife's yell.

In Newcastle upon Tyne cemetery

Here lies Mary, the wife of John Ford,
We hope her soul is gone to the Lord;
But if for Hell she has chang'd this life
She had better be there than be John Ford's wife.

At Potterne cemetery, Wiltshire

This stone was raised to Sarah Ford
Not Sarah's virtues to record
For they're well known by all the town
No, Lord, it was raised to keep her down.

In Kilmory cemetery, Scotland

Here lie my husbands – one, two, three.
Dumb as men could ever be.
As for my fourth, well, praise be God
He bides for a little above the sod.

On the grave of Ivy Saunders in Lancashire

To free me from domestic strife
Death called at my house,
But he spake with my wife.

On a grave in Hadleigh, Suffolk

How fitly joined the lawyer and his wife.
He moved at bar, and she at home, the strife!

Grave of an unknown couple in Somerset

Here let a bard unenvied rest,
Who no dull critic dares molest;
Escaped from the familiar ills
Of threadbare coat and unpaid bills;
From rough bum-bailiff's upstart duns,
From sneering pride's detested sons,
From all those pest'ring ills of life,
From worse than all, a scolding wife.

In Houghton on the Hill churchyard, Leicestershire

The children of Israel wanted bread,
And the Lord he sent them manna,
Old Clerk Wallace wanted a wife,
And the Devil he sent him Anna.

On the grave of John Wallace, Parish Clerk,
of Ribbesford, Bewdley, Hereford

He died in peace
His wife died first.
On a grave in Ilfracombe cemetery, Devon

Beneath this stone and lumps of clay lies
ISABELLA YOUNG
Who, on the 24th of May,
Began to hold her tongue.
From a disappeared grave in the West Midlands

To the Memory of Susan Mum
Silence Is Wisdom
On a grave in Newfield, Durham

Here lies John and with him Mary,
Cheek by jowl and never vary.
No wonder that they so agree,
He wants no punch and she no tea.
From a headstone in Rochdale cemetery, Lancashire

How strange, yet true, that full seventy years
Was his wife happy in her tears!
On the tomb of Daniel Tear at Santon, Cumbria

Here snug in grave my wife doth lie!
Now she's at rest, and so am I.
In Old Greyfriars, Edinburgh

When dear papa went up to Heaven,
What grief mama endured;
And yet that grief was softened, for
Papa was insured.
From a grave in Montreal, Canada

Here lies the man Richard,
And Mary his wife;
Their surname was Pritchard,
They lived without strife;
And the reason is plain –
They abounded in riches,
They had no care or pain,
And his wife wore the britches.

In St Patrick's Church, Dublin

I plant these shrubs upon your grave, dear wife,
That something on this spot may boast of life.
Shrubs must wither and all earth must rot;
Shrubs may revive, but you, thank Heaven, will not.

On a grave in Rhayader, Powys

Charity, wife of Gideon Bligh,
Underneath this stone doth lie,
Naught was she ever known to do
That her husband told her to.

At St Michael Penkevil Church, Devon

Here lies my wife and Heaven knows,
Not less for mine than her repose.

In Plaistow cemetery, London

We lived one and twenty years,
Like man and wife together;
I could no longer have her here,
She's gone – I know not whither.
If I could guess, I do profess
(I speak it not to flatter),
Of all the women in the world,
I never could come at her!
Her body is bestowed well,
A handsome grave doth hide her.
And sure her soul is not in hell –
The Fiend could ne'er abide her!
I think she mounted up on high,
For in the last great thunder,
Methought I heard a voice on high,
Rending the clouds in sunder.

*On the tomb of a lady named Phillips
in Putney, London*

Here lies poor THOMAS DARLING and his wife,
Who led a pretty jarring life;
But all is ended – do you see,
He holds his tongue, and so does she.

From Teignmouth graveyard, Devon

Here lies Margaret Sexton,
Who never did aught to vex one.
Not like the woman under the next stone.

On the grave of a second wife at
Enfield cemetery, Greater London

Stranger, call this not
A Place of Doom,
To me it is a Pleasant Spot,
My Husband's Tomb.

From a disappeared grave in Worcestershire

Underneath this turf doth lie,
Back to back, my wife and I.
Generous stranger, spare the tear,
For could she speak, I cannot hear.
Happier far than when in life,
Free from noise, and free from strife.
When the last trump the air shall fill,
If she gets up, I'll even lie still.

At Halstead Church, Essex

Grieve not for me, my husband dear,
I am not dead, but sleeping here;
With patience wait, prepare to die,
And in a short time you'll come to I.

To which the husband has replied:

I am not grieved, my dearest life;
Sleep on, I have got another wife,
Therefore I cannot come to thee,
For I must go and live with she.

In Hertford cemetery

When Miss Smith was twenty
She had lovers in plenty;
When Miss Smith got older
Her lovers got colder;
Then came Serjeant Spankie
And Miss Smith said thankie.

> *On the grave of Catherine Smith who*
> *beguiled a mean and ageing Scotsman*
> *out of his wealth. In Edinburgh*

To the Memory of
JARED BATES
His widow, aged 24,
lives at 7, Elm Street,
Has every qualification for a Good Wife
And yearns to be comforted.

> *At Aurora Falls, America*

Who far below this tomb doth rest,
Has joined the army of the blest.
The Lord has ta'en her to the sky:
The saints rejoice, and so do I.

> *In Cherening-le-Clay churchyard, Dorset*

Here lies the body of Martha Dias,
Always noisy and not very pious.
Who lived to the age of three score and ten,
And gave to the worms what she refused to men.

From a disappeared grave in Shropshire

Sacred to the memory of Anthony Drake,
Who died for peace and quietness sake,
His wife was constantly scolding and scoffing,
So he sought repose in a twelve dollar coffin.

Burlington, Massachusetts

Oh, cruel Death! Why so unkind,
To take him, and leave me behind?
Better to have taken both or neither,
Which would have been more pleasing to the survivor!

On a woman's grave in St Philip's Church, Birmingham

Here lies JANE SMITH
Wife of THOMAS SMITH, Marble Cutter.
This monument erected by her husband
As a Tribute to her Memory.

Monuments of this style are $250.

From Annapolis cemetery, America

Here lies a woman,
No man can deny it,
She died in peace,
Although she lived unquiet.
Her husband prays,
If e'er this way you walk,
You would tread softly,
If she wakes – she'll talk.

From a disappeared grave in Cumbria

Two great physicians first,
My loving husband tried,
To cure my pain –
In Vain.
At last he got a third,
And then I died.
In Cheltenham churchyard, Gloucestershire

This spot's the sweetest
I've seen in my life
For it raises my flowers
And covers my wife.
In Llanelly cemetery, Gwent

Seven Wives I've buried
With many a fervent prayer:
If we all should meet in heaven
Won't there be trouble there?
From Tyngsboro cemetery, America

Here lies
JOHN GIBBONS
'Peace, perfect Peace'

To which was added on the death of his wife:

'Till We Meet Again'
In Northampton cemetery

She lived with her husband 50 years
And died in the confident hope of a better life.
On a grave in Easingwold Church, Yorkshire

Free from wedlock, care or strife,
He wedded was to single life
To have more spoke he did deserve
But 'twas his will that this should serve.
On the grave of Richard Best, a bachelor,
at Geddington, Northamptonshire

'Tis true I led a single life
And ne'er was married in my life,
For of that sex I ne'er had none:
It is the Lord: his will be done.

From the tomb of William Borrows at
Braunston, Northamptonshire

At threescore winters end I died,
A cheerless being, lone and sad:
The nuptial knot I never tied,
And wished my father never had.

On a gravestone at Saddleworth cemetery,
Greater Manchester

TOMB-STONED

Dead drunk, here Will Elderton doth lie,
Dead as he is, he still is dry;
So of him it may well be said,
Here he, but not his thirst is laid.

> *On the tomb of Will Elderton, 'The Red-Nosed*
> *Ballad Maker', famous for his rhymes*
> *and his drinking, in London*

Jonathan Grober died dead sober.
Lord, Thy Wonders Never Cease.

> *From a grave in San Francisco, America*

Here lies
WILLIAM TEAGUE
Lover of his bottle
Murdered by the meanness of his wife
Chairman of the local Anti-Saloon League
and Dr Amos Throttle.

> *In Greeley graveyard, America*

Beneath this stone Tom Cobbold lies,
He cares not now who laughs or cries.
He laughed when sober and when mellow,
A heedless, harum-scarum fellow.
He gave to none designed offence,
So honi soit qui mal y pense.

In Hendon cemetery, London

Here sleeps in peace a Hampshire grenadier,
Who caught his death by drinking cold, small beer.
Soldiers! Take heed from his untimely fall,
And when you're hot, drink strong, or none at all!

To which was later added:

An honest soldier never is forgot,
Whether he die by musket or by pot.

On the grave of Thomas Fletcher in Winchester

Enclosed within this narrow stall,
Lies one who was a friend to **awl.**
He saved bad **soles** from getting worse,
But damned his own without remorse,
And though a drunken life he passed,
Yet saved **his sole,** by **mending at the last.**

On the grave of John Peters,
a drunken cobbler of Manchester

He had some faults,
And many merits,
He died of drinking,
Ardent spirits.

From a headstone in New Orleans
cemetery, America

Life is an Inn, where all men bait,
The waiter Time, the Landlord Fate;
Death is the score by all men due,
I've paid my shot, and so must you.

On a tombstone in Mickleham, Surrey

Hark, this stone doth mark the spot,
Where a notorious sot doth lie;
Whether at rest or not,
It matters not to you or I!
Oft to the 'Lion' he went to fill his horn
Now to the 'Grave' he's gone to get it warm.

From a disappeared gravestone in
Tunbridge Wells, Kent

Here lies John Steere,
Who, when living, brewed good beer,
Turn to the right, go down the hill,
His son keeps up the business still.

In Dagenham cemetery, Essex

In life a jovial sot was he,
He died from inebriety.
A cup of burnt sack,
To Earth from Heaven would bring him back.

On landlord John Webb in Cheshire

Here lies the Landlord of 'The Lion',
He hopes removed to the lands of Sion,
His wife, resigned to Heaven's will,
Will carry on the business still.

To which was added two years later:

Here lies the Landlord's loving wife,
Her soul removed from lands of strife.
She's gone aloft her spouse to tell
The Inn he left her turned out well.

In Bideford churchyard, Devon

A jolly landlord once was I
And kept the Old King's Head hard by
Sold mead and gin, cider and beer,
And eke all other kinds of cheer,
Till Death my licence took away,
And put me in this house of clay:
A house at which you all must call,
Sooner or later, great or small.

On a tombstone in Roughtonhead
Parish Church, Cumbria

Here lies Walter Gunn,
Sometimes landlord of the Tun;
Sic transit gloria mundi!
He drank hard upon Friday
That being a high day,
Then took to his bed and died upon Sunday.

On a North Country landlord's grave

Though hot my name, yet mild my nature,
I bore good will to every creature;
I brewed good ale and sold it too,
And unto each I gave his due.

On the grave of William Pepper at
St John's, Stamford

In Memory of Rebecca Freeland,
She drank good ale, good punch and wine
And lived to the age of 99.

On a grave in Edwallon cemetery,
Nottinghamshire

Bacchus, to give the toping world surprise
Produced one sober son, and here he lies.
Tho' nursed among full hogsheads, he defied
The charm of wine, and every vice beside.

On Robert Preston, a landlord, at
St Michael's, Eastcheap, who died aged 27!

'Twas as she tript from cask to cask,
In at a bung-hole she quickly fell,
Suffocation was her task,
She had no time to say farewell.

On the grave of barmaid Ann Collins
at King's Stanley, Gloucestershire

Poor JOHN SCOTT lies buried here,
Although he was both hale and stout;
Death stretched him on the bitter bier,
Now in another world he hops about.

In St George's Parish Church, Liverpool

Dead drunk old Susan oft was found;
But now she's laid beneath the ground,
As door-nail dead - alas the day!
Her nose was red, and moist as clay.
From morn to night, of care bereft,
She plied her glass, and wet her throttle,
Without a sigh her friends she left
But much she griev'd to leave her bottle.

On a disappeared grave of Susan Webster
in Somerset

Beneath the droppings of this spout,
Here lies the body once so stout
of FRANCIS THOMPSON
The Rufford's records can declare,
His action who, for seven year,
Both drew and drank its potent beer.
Here rest good shade, nor hell nor vermin fear,
Thy virtues guard thy soul,
And thy body good strong beer.

On the tombstone of Francis Thompson,
in Ollerton churchyard, Cheshire

Here lyes – read it with your hats on
The Bones of Bailie William Watson,
Who was moderate in his thinking,
And famous for his drinking.

On the monument to a Glasgow magistrate

John Adams lies here, of the parish of Southwell
A carrier who carried his can to his mouth well;
He carried so much, and he carried so fast,
He could carry no more – so was carried at last!
For the liquor he drunk, being too much for one,
He could not carry-off – so he's now carri-on.

On a gravestone in Southwell cemetery, Dorset

Here old John Randell lies, who, telling of his tale,
Lived threescore years and ten, such virtue was in ale:
Ale was his meat; ale was his drink; ale did his heart
   revive;
And if he could have drunk his ale, he still had been
   alive.

At St Benet's Church, Muswell Hill, London

Here lies JOHNNY PIGEON
Strong ale was his ablution,
Small beer persecution,
A dram was memento mori;
But a full flowing bowl
Was the saving of his soul,
And port was celestial glory!

On the grave of John Dove at Mauchline, Strathclyde

Who lies here? Who do'e think?
Why, old Clapper Watts, if you'll give him some drink
Give a dead man drink? For why?
Why when he was alive he was always a-dry.

On the grave of Clarence Watts
in Leigh Delamere churchyard, Wiltshire

Here lie the bones of Donald Jones,
The wale of men for eating scones;
Eating scones and drinking ale,
Till his last moans he took his fill.

In Skye cemetery, Scotland

DEATH-INITIONS

Here, Reader, you may plainly see,
That wit nor humour can be proof
against mortality.
On a grave at Mancroft Church, Norwich, Norfolk

Here lies the wife of Simon Stokes,
Who lived and died – like other folks.
In Stratford cemetery, London

A heap of stones you see appear,
For why? Because Sir Harry lieth here.
*On the monument of Sir Henry
Coningsby in Gwent*

Here lieth Sir Thomas Jay, Knight,
Who, being dead, I upon his grave did shite.
Discovered on a grave at Poole, Dorset

Here lies the good old knight Sir Harry,
Who loved well, but would not marry.
On the grave of an amorous man at
Ditchley churchyard, Oxford

Here lies Sir John Plumpudding of the Grange,
Who hanged himself one morning for a change.
From a disappeared grave in Northumberland

Here lies the corpse of Dr Chard
Who filled up half of this churchyard.
On the grave of Thomas Chard in Yeovil, Somerset

Here lies my adviser, Dr Sim,
And those he healed – near him.
In Grimsby Parish Church, Humberside

Here lies the body of Thomas Proctor,
Who lived and died without a doctor.

On a headstone in Luton cemetery,
Bedfordshire

Here lies Stephen Rumbold, who lived to 101,
Sanguine & Strong,
An hundred to one you don't live so long!

In Brightwell Baldwin churchyard, Oxfordshire

He lived and died,
By suicide.

On the grave of a Coroner who hanged
himself at West Grinstead, London

Visitors tread gently
Here lies Doctor Bentley.

In Great Haywood churchyard, Staffordshire

Here lies Lawyer Smith, and what is something rarish,
He was born, bred, and hanged in the selfsame parish.

On the grave of Thomas Smith in Cumbria

God works a wonder now and then,
Here, though a lawyer, was an honest man.

In Pineton churchyard, Norfolk

Beneath this turf a man doth lie,
Who dyed to live, and lived to die.

*On the tomb of John Calcross, a dyer,
of Lavenham, Suffolk*

Lie **heavy** on him earth, for he
Laid many a **heavy** load on thee.

*On Sir John Vanbrugh, architect, in
St Stephen's, Chiswick, London*

Stephen and Time are now both even,
Stephen beats Time, but now Time's beating Stephen.

On the headstone of a musician
at St Ives, Cornwall

Stranger, tread this ground with gravity,
Dentist Brown is filling his last cavity.

On a tomb in St George's Church, Edinburgh

Here lies John Trott, by trade a bum;
When he died the devil cry'd – Come, John, come.

On the grave of John Trott, a bailiff
of Hackney, London

Here lies the remains of John Hall, Grocer,
The world is not worth a **fig** and I have good
raisins for saying so!

In Dunmore churchyard, Ireland

Here I lies
Killed by the XIS.
The grave of a smuggler in Woodbridge, Suffolk

Foote from this earthly stage, alas! is hurled;
Death took him off who took off all the world.
On the tomb of comedian
Samuel Foote in London

Hurrah! my boys, at the Parson's fall,
For if he'd lived, he'd a-buried us all!
In Taibach churchyard, W. Glamorgan

Reader, if cash thou art in want of any,
Dig five feet deep and you will find a PENNY.
On the grave of Thomas Penny in
Witnesham Parish Church, Suffolk

Here lies Old Father Gripe, who never cried 'I am satis';
'Twould wake him did he know you read his tombstone
  gratis.

On the grave of a miser in Glasgow

Here lyeth Father Sparges,
That dyed to save the charges.

In Camden cemetery, London

Poems and epitaphs are but stuff,
Here lies Bob Barras and that's enough.

On a headstone in Croydon cemetery, Surrey

He is not here, but only his pod;
He shelled out his peas and went to his God.

*On the grave of Zekiel Peace
in Nantucket, America*

Here lieth Richard Dent,
In his last tenement.

At Finedon, Northamptonshire

Here lies John Ross,
Kicked by a Hoss.

On a grave in Kendal Parish Church, Cumbria

Here lies the body of Johnny Denholm,
If ye saw him noo, Ye widnae ken him.

From a grave in Glasgow

See what Death with spade hath donen to wee,
Having new planted both bud, branch and tree.

On the tomb of the Wood family
in Marnhull churchyard, Dorset

Death will'd that **Willing** here should lie,
Although unwilling he to die.

> *On the grave of William Willing at Lincoln*

True to his King, his country was his glory,
When Bony won, he said it was a story.

> *On the headstone of a patriot*
> *at Kirk Hallam cemetery, Derbyshire*

Some have children, some have none;
Here lies the mother of 21.

> *On the headstone of Ann Jennings,*
> *in Wolstanston cemetery, Cheshire*

Here lie mother and babe both without sins
Next birth will make her and her infant twins.
On the wife of a Dr Wilkinson,
at Great Milton, Oxfordshire

John Calf junior lieth here
Without becoming Ox or Steer.
On the Calf family tomb at Cheriton
Parish Church, Winchester

CEMETARIANS

CAPTAIN TULLY

Here lies the body of Captain Tully,
Aged a hundred and nine years fully;
And threescore years before, as mayor,
The sword of this city he did bear.
Nine of his wives do by him lie,
So shall the tenth when she doth die!

On the tomb of John Tully,
a mayor of Exeter, Devon

NICHOLAS TOKE

Five times he wived
But still survived;
To seek a sixth he,
At the age of 93
Walked to London Town;
But the journey
Got him down.

From a headstone in Kensington
cemetery, London

ANN MANN

Here lies Ann Mann
She lived an old maid
And died an old Mann.

In Barton Moss cemetery, nr. Manchester

MEREDITH MORGAN

Under this stone lies Meredith Morgan,
Who blew the bellows of our Church Organ;
Tobacco he hated, to smoke most unwilling,
Yet never so pleased as when pipes he was filling;
No reflection on him for rude speech could be cast,
Tho' he gave our old organist many a blast.
No puffer was he
Tho' a capital blower;
He could fill double G
And now lies a note lower.

In Llanfihangel Tal-y-ilyn churchyard, Powys

DOLL PENTREATH

Old Doll Pentreath, one hundred age and two,
Both born, and in Paul Parish, buried too;
Not in the Church 'mongst people great and high,
But in the Churchyard doth Old Dollie lie!

On a grave in St Paul's churchyard,
Mousehole, Cornwall

JOHN AND RUTH WARREN

Here under this stone
Lie Ruth and old John,
Who smoked all his life
And so did his wife.
And now there's no doubt
But their pipes are both out.
Be it said without joke
That life is but smoke,
Though we live to fourscore
'Tis a whiff and no more.

On a grave in Marnhull, Dorset.
John Warren lived to the age of 94!

DOCTOR IVAN LETSOME

When people's ill they come to I,
I physics, bleeds, and sweats 'em;
Sometimes they live, sometimes they die;
What's that to I? I Letsome.

In San Francisco, America

JAMES WILSON

Here lies what's left of Lawyer Wilson,
Who, some folks say, died mad at Bilston!
But others say 'twas not so bad
Who ever knew a fool go mad?

In Bilston cemetery, Lothian

JONATHAN THOMPSON

A good Husband and affectionate Father
Whose disconsolate Widow and Orphans
Continue to carry on the Tripe and Trotter business
At the same shop as before their bereavement.

From Shoreditch graveyard, London

GEORGE LAMB

Beneath this stone lies Lamb asleep,
Who died a lamb and lived a sheep.
Many a lamb and sheep he slaughtered,
But butcher death the scene has altered.

From the grave of a Spitalfields butcher, London

NELL BATCHELOR

Beneath this dust lies the smouldering crust
Of Eleanor Batchelor's shoven,
Well versed in the arts of pies, puddings and tarts
And the lucrative trade of the oven.
When she'd lived long enough,
She made her last puff,
A puff by her husband much praised,
And now she doth lie and makes a dirt pie
And hopes that her crust will be raised.

On the grave of an Oxford pie-maker

CATHERINE GRAY

Beneath this stone lies Catherine Gray,
Changed to a lifeless lump of clay;
By earth and clay she got her wealth,
And now she's turned to earth herself.
Ye weeping friends, let me advise,
Abate your tears and dry your eyes;
For what avails a flood of tears?
Who knows but in a course of years,
In some tall pitcher or brown pan,
She in her shop may be again!

On the grave of crockery dealer
Catherine Gray, in Chester

DAVID WINTER

Here lies Mr Winter, collector of taxes,
I'd advise you to pay him whatever he axes;
Excuses won't do, he stands no sort of flummery,
Tho' Winter his name is, his process is summary.

In Eastcheap graveyard, London

MULCIBER GRIM

Here **cool** the **ashes** of Mulciber Grim.
From his youth upwards he was much addicted
   to **vices**, and was often guilty of **forgery**.
Having some talents for **irony**,
   he therefore produced many **heats** in his neighbourhood,
Which he usually increased by **blowing up the coals**.
At length, after passing a long life in the commission of
   these **black actions**, his **fire** being exhausted,
   and his **bellows** worn out,
He filed off to that place where only the **fervid ordeal** of
   his own **forge** can be exceeded:
Declaring, with his last **puff**, that man is born to trouble
   as the **sparks** fly upwards.

        On the tomb of a blacksmith in Ongar, Essex

DICK MARSHALL

Here lies Dick, a baker by trade,
Who was always in business praised;
And here snug he lies, in his oven, 'tis said,
In hopes that his bread may be raised.

        In Teddington cemetery, London

ROBERT TROLLOPE

Here lies Robert Trollope,
Who made these stones roll up;
When death took his soul up,
His body filled this hole up.

On the grave of a Newcastle architect at
Gateshead, Co. Durham

GERVASE SCROPE

Here lies an Old Toss'd Tennis Ball,
Was Racketted from Spring to Fall
With so much heat and so much blast
Time's arm (for shame) grew tyr'd at last.

On a tennis enthusiast in Coventry
cemetery, Warwickshire

JAMES BARKER

Here lies the Conqueror conquered,
Valiant as ever England bred;
Whom neither art, nor steel, nor strength
Could e'er subdue, till death at length
Threw him on his back and here he lies
In hopes hereafter to arise.

The grave of a wrestling champion
in Bluntisham, Cambridge

NATHANIEL HALL

I bowl'd, I struck, I stopp'd,
Sure life's a game of cricket,
I blocked with care, with caution popp'd,
Yet death has hit my wicket.

*The monument to a keen cricketer
in Salisbury cemetery, Wiltshire*

POKER JIM WILKINS

To the memory of
Poker Jim Wilkins
His Last Full House.

In Morrisburg cemetery, America

THOMAS KEMP

Here lies the body of Thomas Kemp,
Who lived by wool and died by hemp;
There's nothing would suffice this glutton,
But with the fleece to steal the mutton;
Had he but worked and lived uprighter,
He'd ne'er been hung for a sheep-biter.

In Bellingham Parish churchyard, Northumberland

JAMES LOCK
Here lies the body of
'Arkansaw Jim'
We made the mistake
But the joke's on him.

*In Culver City, America. Erected by
the Vigilante Committee*

BILL THOMSON
Here Lies Pecos Bill
He always lied
And he always will.
He once lied loud
And now lies still.

On a tombstone in Grand Forks, America

ELLEN GEE

Peerless yet hapless maid of Q,
Accomplished L N G,
Never again shall I and U
Together Sip our T.

For, ah! the fates I know not Y,
Sent midst the flowers a B,
Which ven'mous stung her in the I,
So that she could not C.

Ye nymphs of Q, then shun each B,
List to the reason Y,
For should a B C U at T,
He'll surely sting your I.

Now in a grave L deep in Q,
She's cold as cold can B,
Whilst robins sing upon A U,
Her dirge and L E G.

On the grave of a woman who died
of a bee sting in Kew, Surrey

CHARLES KNOTT
Here lies a man that was Knott born,
His father was Knott before him.
He lived Knott, and did Knott die;
Yet underneath this stone doth lie,
Knott christened,
Knott begot,
And here he lies,
And yet was Knott.

On a grave in Bromsgrove, Worcestershire

PHILIP BOX
Here lies one Box within another,
The one of wood was very good,
We cannot say so much for t'other.

On a headstone in Leeds cemetery, Yorkshire

JOHN FISH
Worms bait for fish;
But here's a sudden change.
Fish's bait for worms,
Is that not passing strange?

On a disappeared grave in Cumbria

MARTIN ELPHINSTONE

Here lieth Martin Elphinstone,
Who with his sword did cut in sunder,
The daughter of Sir Harry Crispe.
She was fat and fulsome,
But men will sometimes
Eat bacon with their bean,
And love the fat as well as lean.

In Alnwick cemetery, Northumberland

TEAGUE O'BRIEN

Here I at length repose,
My spirit now at aise is,
With the tips of my toes,
And the point of my nose,
Turned up to the roots of the daisies.

In Ballypooren churchyard, Ireland

WILLIAM WRAY

Here lieth wrapt in clay,
The body of William Wray
I have no more to say.

On a memorial stone in Shropshire

MATTHEW MUD
Here lies Matthew Mud,
Death did him no hurt.
When alive he was **Mud**,
And now dead he's but dirt.

On a grave in Watton churchyard, Norfolk

JEMMY WYATT
At rest beneath this churchyard stone,
Lies stingy Jemmy Wyatt;
He died one morning just at ten,
And saved a dinner by it!

On a disappeared grave in Studley churchyard,
Wiltshire

LETTUCE MANNING
Oh, Cruel Death,
To satisfy thy palate,
Cut down our Lettuce,
To make a salad.

In Moulton churchyard, Cambridgeshire

JOSHUA HIGHT

Beneath this plain board is lying
The body of Joshua Hight
'Cheer up,' the parson told him, dying,
'Your future's very bright.'

Slowly the sick man raised his head,
His weeping friends amazing.
'Parson, it's most too bright,' he said.
'For I can see it blazing!'

On a tomb in Boston, Massachusetts

WILLIAM JONES

Here lie the bones of William Jones,
Who, when alive, collected bones.
But Death, that bony, grisly spectre,
That most amazing bone collector,
Has boned poor Jones so snug and tidy,
That here he lies in **bona fide.**

On a disappeared grave in Plaistow, London

MARTHA GWYNN

Sacred to the memory of Miss Martha Gwynn,
Who was so very pure within
She burst the outer shell of sin,
And hatch'd herself a cherubim.

St Albans cemetery, Hertfordshire

MELANTHA GRIBBLING

The dust of
Melantha Gribbling
Swept up at last
by the Great Housekeeper

On a grave in Woodville, America

JOHN RACKETT

Here lies John Rackett, in his wooden jacket:
Kept neither horses nor mules,
Lived a Hog – Died a Dog.
Left all his money to fools.

In Belgarave cemetery, America

PAMELA LEE

In her life she did her best,
Now I hope her soul's at rest;
Also her son, Tom, lies at her feet –
He lived till he made both ends meet.

On the memorial to a woman and her son at
Frindsbury, Kent

PETER ROBINSON

Here lies the preacher, judge
And poet, Peter:
Who broke the laws of God and Man
And metre.

On a headstone in Bristol cemetery, Avon

JOHN ELDRED

Here lies the body of John Eldred,
At least he will be here when he is dead;
But now at this time he is alive,
The 14th of August, sixty five.

On a disappeared tombstone in Oxfordshire

NATHANIEL FREER

My name it was Nathaniel Freer,
I lived and laughed, but now I'm here.
Such as I am, such you must be,
So make your game, and follow me!
On a grave in Elsham cemetery, Northamptonshire

And finally:

THOMAS DE'ATH

Death levels all, both high and low,
Without regard to stations;
Yet why complain
If **we** are slain?
For here lies one at least to show
He kills his own relations!

From the grave of a relative of the author's
in Huddersfield, Yorkshire

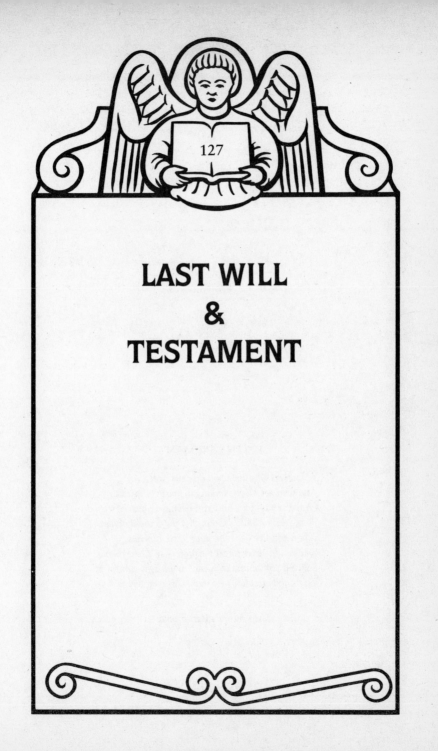

127

LAST WILL
&
TESTAMENT

For

KEITH LARKMAN

Ye lawyers who live upon litigants' fees,
And who need a good many to live at your ease;
Grave or gay, wise or witty, whate'er your degree,
Plain stuff or State's Counsel, take counsel of me:
When a festive occasion your spirit unbends,
You should never forget the profession's best friends:
So we'll send round the wine, and a light bumper fill
To the jolly testator who makes his own will.

The Lawyer's Best Friend

PREFACE

Every family has a story which each generation dies to tell – or alternatively that they tell of the deceased. For most of those skeletons that (figuratively speaking) rattle around in family cupboards are reminders of something in a forebear's life they would probably prefer to have kept in the dark. When you enjoy a name like mine – and you have to enjoy it the best way you can – it's perhaps only to be expected that such a story should be about a moment of farewell to the world and all its troubles. And because it's rather to do with the business of making a will, I'd like to tell it here. It's quite amusing, too – or it strikes me so.

The story concerns an aged female relative who died at the turn of the century. The old lady was apparently a bit of a hypochondriac as well as being quite wealthy. As she lay dying, she summoned the members of the family to her home, along with her doctor who for years she had never failed to call out on the slightest excuse. It was thought, however, I must add, that he would receive a quite substantial bequest in her will when she made it, and this doubtless encouraged him when he wearily made his way to her door once again.

When the doctor arrived for what was to prove his last visit, the old lady sent her relatives (mine, that is) from the room, and called the good man to her bedside. She wanted to talk to him on a serious matter, she said in a fading voice. Though not an avaricious man by nature, the doctor couldn't help wondering if she was going to make her will now, and that he might just be in for a little something.

'Doctor . . .,' she began, 'I've . . . given . . . you . . .'

Before the old lady could go on, the man hurriedly raised his hand. If she *was* about to make her last testament, he wanted a witness or two on hand.

'Just a moment,' he said, about to get up and go to the door. 'I had better call in your family.'

The old lady seemed not to have heard him.

'I've given you,' she repeated in a voice now little more than a whisper, 'given . . . you . . . a . . . great . . . deal . . . of trouble!'

And with that she fell back on her pillow and breathed her last.

Few people, of course, leave it to the very last moment to make a will, but that old lady was by no means unusual in giving someone a laugh when she died. Now, no one would suggest that the business of dying was amusing, but because we can't take it with us – whatever *it* may be – we have to do something with what we're leaving behind. And that's where the will to find a way comes in.

Solicitors, being the naturally reserved gentlemen (and women) they are, encourage people to make the most formal wills, leaving nothing to chance. But sometimes that old devil chance is precisely what some people *want* to leave it to. I mean they would rather see a smile on someone's face as a result of their last instructions, or else they use their final testament as an opportunity to have the last word on someone

who may have been having it at their expense all their life. Indeed, I'm rather in sympathy with what the famous essayist, William Hazlitt, had to say on the matter of 'Will-making'.

'Few things show the human character in a more ridiculous light than the circumstances of will-making,' he wrote in his book, *Table Talk* (1821).

> It is the latest opportunity we have of exercising the natural perversity of the disposition, and we take care to make a good use of it. We husband it with jealousy, put it off as long as we can, and then use every precaution that the world shall be no gainer by our deaths. This last act of our lives seldom belies the former tenor of them, for stupidity, caprice, and unmeaning spite. All that we seem to think of is to manage matters so (in settling accounts with those who are so unmannerly as to survive us) as to do as little good and to plague and disappoint as many people as possible.

Hazlitt, in particular, saw the will as a means of frustrating the expectations of people who had been servile and selfish merely in the hope of reaping a financial benefit – thus, he said, 'the cringing toad-eater, the officious tale-bearer, is perhaps well paid for years of obsequious attendance with a bare mention and a mourning ring.'

There have been, however, over the years, a great many people who have received much more than a bare mention,

and sometimes a lot less than a mourning ring, from departed relatives, friends or what-have-yous. And the proof of this largesse (or lack of it) lies in the collection of wills which are herein presented for your interest and amusement. To assemble them I have researched sources all over the world, and the examples range from the earliest periods of history right up to the present day.

The art of will-making is, in fact, of considerable antiquity: and those who have used the opportunity of their final testament to right a wrong or wrong a right bad'un have been in evidence for most of this time. One legend has it that Noah made the first will – generously dividing up the entire world three ways with his sons – while some historians feel the Egyptians originated the practice. The wily Orientals were certainly busy bequeathing their property in like manner long before the birth of Christ, and similarly the Greeks – though we all know the stories about Greeks bearing gifts . . .

But in a light-hearted collection of last wills and testaments such as this, origins need not particularly concern us. It is the words and the intentions that we are interested in, and again I am reminded of some lines written by the humorist Jerome K. Jerome who reached two conclusions after years of studying the business of will-making. The first, he said, was that if a man died *without* leaving a will, then all his property went to the nearest villain. Secondly, that if a man *did* leave a will then everything he owned went to whoever could get

possession of that will! William Hazlitt would have approved those remarks, I think!

The wills I have gathered range from the amazing to the absurd, from the ridiculous to the incredible, and from the farcical to the satirical. Whether they concern a husband maligning a nagging wife, a wife getting even with a heartless husband, one relative settling an old score with another, or just an act of humorous generosity to man or beast (for even our dumb friends have had their fair share of bequests) you can be sure about one thing. Every one of these wills is genuine – you have my word on that!

Richard De'ath
September 1983

1

JUST A BEQUEST IN TIME

The earliest existing will containing a touch of humour
was written about AD 156 by the eccentric,
impoverished philosopher, Eudamidas of Corinth. It was
actually preserved by the Greek writer, Lucian, who, of
course, was responsible for producing a new form of
Literature – humorous dialogue. Apparently, on account of
his poverty, Eudamidas had very little he could bequeath to
his two closest friends, Arethaeus and Charixenes, and
indeed what he *did* give them many people might think of
dubious worth:

'I bequeath to Arethaeus my mother to support; and I
pray him to have a tender care of her declining years.
 'I bequeath to Charixenes my daughter to marry, and to
give her to that end the best portion he can afford.
 'Should either happen to die, I beg the other to
undertake both charges.'

The Marquis du Chatelet, an eccentric French nobleman
of Neufchateau requested that he be buried in the
following manner in his will dated 1280:

'*Item.* That one of the pillars in the church at
Neufchateau be hollowed out and my body placed
therein, in order that the vulgar may not walk upon me.'

A funeral that was more like a festival was requested by Signor Lodovico Cortusio, the Consul of Padua in Italy, in his will of July 1418:

'I forbid that any of my relatives or friends should weep at my funeral; any of those found so doing shall be disinherited. While, on the other hand, he who shall laugh most heartily shall be my principal heir and universal legatee.

'I desire to be conducted to the church by musicians who will play most joyfully. My body is to be enclosed in a bier covered with a cloth of divers colours and carried by twelve young girls habited in green also singing cheerful and lively songs.

'I further order that no clergy or monk dressed in black should attend, all should come in light-coloured costumes or refrain from attending in order not to sadden the spectacle by the appearance of mourning.'

Johann Ziska, the extraordinary blind chieftain of the Hussites, made a grim though not altogether humourless request in his will of 1424:

'Immediately after my death I require that my body be flayed, my skin preserved and tanned, and from this a drum-head made. The noise of such a drum will alone suffice to scare the enemies of the tribe and to preserve to it all the advantages I have obtained for it.'

(Remarkably, this strange request has a modern-day counterpart given later in this book.)

An Italian priest with a renowned sense of fun called 'Arlotto, the Parson', left instructions in his will dated 1483 that the following words were to be inscribed on his tomb:

'This sepulchre was made by the parson Arlotto for himself - and for any other man who may desire to enter therein.'

Anxious to promote peace and harmony among mankind, Robert Halliday of Eastcheap, London in his will of May 1491 bequeathed the sum of £5 annually to the churchwardens with these instructions:

'Either to make an entertainment among such persons of his home parish of St Clement, who should be at variance with each other, in the week preceding Easter, to induce such persons to be better neighbours and to

begat brotherly love amongst them; or if none should be found in the said parish, then to make an entertainment with the said money at the tavern amongst the honest parishioners of the said parish on the day common called Shere Thursday, that they may pray more fervently.'

The aptly named Alice Love of Rye in Sussex lived up to her name when she came to make her will in 1506, bequeathing several items of jewellery and clothing to her young lovers, including one very special bequest:

'And to Thomas Oxenbridge, my best girdle, which bound me but never denied him.'

The Duchess of Northumberland, however, was clearly a very shy woman as her will of 1536 reveals in these amusing lines:

'In nowise let me be opened after I am dead; I have not used to be very bold before women, much more would I be loth to come into the hands of any living man, be he physician or surgeon.'

The French satirist, François Rabelais (1494–1553) wrote with typical humour in the will he made in 1550:

'I have no available property, I owe a great deal, and the rest I give to the poor.'

Among the strangest instructions for burial must be those found in the will of an unknown Frenchman, buried in Poitevin in 1595, and quoted by the historian P. Garasse:

'And I order that my body shall be enveloped in a tanned pig-skin, and buried perpendicularly before the high altar of the church, on a pile of charcoal, for there is no other god in the world than the incorruptibility of the body, and that charcoal and tanned leather are two agents sufficiently powerful to prevent putrefaction.'

(That this man was something of a humorist may be judged by the fact that he requested that this funeral be 'conducted with every species of mirth and hilarity', and his mourners should carry laurel branches instead of tapers. A further clause that anyone who attended his funeral could have whatever coin and jewels he found in a vault in the man's home was unfortunately frustrated, for his servants heard about this before the funeral and swiftly removed the whole lot!)

Apart from being the greatest of our playwrights, William Shakespeare was also a man of wit, as this extract from his will made in Stratford-upon-Avon in 1616 reveals:

'**Item. I give unto my wife my second-best bed, with the furniture.**'

(*It was Shakespeare's daughters, Susanna and Judith, who received his best bed – along with most of the rest of his furniture, property and wealth.*)

The humorous Italian writer, Alessandro Tassoni, could not resist a joke or two in his will of 1612, declaring that he was 'sound in body and mind, save and except that singular fever which torments all human beings and makes them wish to survive their deaths'. He continued:

'**My wish would be that my funeral should only employ one priest, that there should be simply the small cross and a single candle, and that as regards expense no more shall be incurred than will pay for a sack to stuff my remains into, and a porter to carry it.**

'**I bequeath to the parish in which I may be buried twelve gold crowns, without the smallest condition; the gift appearing to me very trifling, and, moreover, that I only give it because I cannot carry it away.**

'And to my natural son named Marzio, whose mother is a certain Lucia of Garfagnano, I leave a hundred crowns in carlinos, that he may dissipate them at the wine-shop.'

Jasper Mayne, described as a 'punster' of London, had apparently been served for much of his life by a valet who was more often drunk than sober. In his will he repaid this feckless servant in a manner that must have given him cause to chuckle as he drew up his instructions in 1620:

'*Item.* To my valet, B . . . , my old portmanteau, which oft I carried when he should have, not so much for its own value, as for its contents, there being within something that will enable him to drink. This I give with right good spirits.'

(*No doubt hoping to find a bottle or two inside the old case, the valet opened his master's legacy with eager anticipation – only to discover in it nothing but a red herring!*)

Philip, the Earl of Pembroke and a supporter of King Charles, took a violent dislike to the author of a book about Oliver Cromwell, and remembered the man in these amusing words from his will of 1657:

'*Item.* I bequeath to Thomas May, whose nose I did break at a masquerade, five shillings. My intention had been to give him more; but all who shall have seen his *History of the Parliament* will consider that even this sum is too large.'

A curious bequest for a sport outlawed in England was made in the will of George Staverton of Wokingham, Berkshire in May 1661:

'I hereby bequeath from my estate a yearly sum of £6 to buy a bull, which bull I give to the poor of Wokingham town and parish that it may be baited. Having been killed, the hide and offal are to be sold, and with any money remaining from the gift after the purchase of the bull, bestowed upon the poor children of the town and parish for stockings and shoes.'

There was a catch in Thomas Walker's bequest to help some of the poor people of Bristol in his will of April 1666:

'I give and bequeath to that poor parish of St James the sum of £200, to purchase for ever the sum of £10 8s 0d a year for eight poor house-keepers that are known to live in the fear of God, and to come into the church every Lord's day – but for God's sake let them be no drunkards nor common swearers.'

Valentine Goodman, a resident of Hallton, Leicestershire, was a man who lived up to his name, though his choice of words to describe those who were to benefit from his bequest made in 1684 was certainly not the most tactful:

'I bequeath the sum of £800 to be laid out in land and the profits therefrom given each year to the most indigent, poorest, aged, decrepit, miserable paupers of the district. And I decree that if any part of the money is employed for easing town levies, or not according to the intent of my bequest, then the gift must cease and the money employed for the redemption of Turkish captives.'

The wild and promiscuous life of his French wife, Charlotte, caused Henry, the Earl of Stafford, who was exiled with James II at the end of the seventeenth century, to declare in his will:

'To the worst of women, Claude Charlotte de Grammont,

unfortunately my wife, guilty as she is of all crimes, I leave five-and-forty brass halfpence, which will buy a pullet for her supper. A better gift than her father can make her; for I have known when, having not the money, neither had he the credit for such a purchase; he being the worst of men, and his wife the worst of women, in all debaucheries. Had I known their characters I would never have married their daughter, and made myself unhappy.'

John Cobbet, a Hertfordshire farmer, gave these hilarious instructions to his family in his will of 1720:

'It is my wish as I am about to take a thirty years nap, that my coffin should be suspended from a beam in my barn and not nailed down. The coffin may be locked, only so long as a hole is made in the side through which the key may be pushed so that I can let myself out when I awake.'

(Records indicate that farmer Cobbet's instructions were carried out, but when in 1750 he failed to 'awake' his nephew, Peter, allowed him another year's grace, and then decently buried the coffin in the ground!)

Another person who well lived up to his nickname was 'Mad' Jack Fuller, a country squire of Brightling in Sussex who devoted his life to devising crazy schemes, drinking with his cronies or else hunting with falcons. In his will of 1743 he managed to combine all these interests in one last bizarre idea:

'I desire not to be buried in the ground, but walled up in a large stone tomb, my body seated in an upright position. And to keep me company, a bottle and a bird placed by my side.'

A devout old churchgoer, John Rudge of Trysull, Staffordshire, who had evidently witnessed the offences which he left a bequest to prevent, wrote in his will of 17 April, 1725:

'*Item.* I do also bequeath the sum of twenty shillings a year, payable at five shillings a quarter, to a poor man to go about the parish church of Trysull, during sermon, to keep people awake, and to keep dogs out of the church.'

Hatred towards a neighbour was clearly expressed by John Swain of Southwark, London, who made this bequest in his will of 1765:

'*Item.* To my neighbour, John Abbot, and Mary his wife, sixpence each, to buy for them a noose, for fear the sheriffs should not be provided.'

Dennis Tolam, a somewhat comical Irishman who lived in Cork, was believed to have hoarded away a fortune during his lifetime, which naturally aroused great interest among his relatives when his will was read in 1769. Their initial excitement, however, began to dwindle as the old man's 'bequests' were declared:

'*Item.* I leave to my sister-in-law four old stockings which will be found under my mattress, to the right.
'*Item.* To my nephew, Michael Tarles, two odd socks and a green nightcap.
'*Item.* To Lieutenant John Stein, a blue stocking with my red cloak.
'*Item.* To my cousin, Barbara Dolan, an old boot with a red flannel pocket.
'*Item.* To Hannah, my housekeeper, my broken water jug.'

(*As the disappointed heirs were about to leave the room, the housekeeper Hannah indignantly dropped the old water jug. It cracked open to reveal a hoard of coins. And when the others carefully examined their 'bequests' each in turn found large sums of money concealed inside. The comic had had his last laugh!*)

A man interested in the furtherance of marriage as well as horse racing made this peculiar bequest in his will dated 30 May, 1772. John Perram of Newmarket, England declared that his estate was to be realised so that:

'A marriage portion of £20 may be given to a parishioner of this parish who on Thursday in the Easter week, be married at the church to a woman belonging to it; neither party to be under twenty, nor to exceed twenty-five years of age, nor be worth £20; the trustees to attend in the vestry to receive claims and pay the bequest to such couples as should be qualified to receive it.

'In the case of no claimants, then the money, for that year only, to be paid by the trustees to the winner of the next town horse-race; the race course at Newmarket is four miles long and is regarded the finest in the world.'

Quite the reverse attitude was taken by an English
nobleman, Lord Chesterfield, who had a godson evidently
addicted to gambling on the horses, for he inserted this
punishing clause in his will of 1773:

'In case my said godson, Philip Stanhome, shall, at any
time hereafter keep, or be concerned in keeping of, any
racehorse, or pack of hounds, or reside one night at
Newmarket, that infamous seminary of iniquity and
ill-manners, during the course of races there; or shall
resort to the said races, or shall lose, in any one day, at
any game or bet whatsoever, the sum of £500; then, in
any of the cases aforesaid, it is my express will that he,
my said godson, shall forfeit and pay out of my estate the
sum of £5,000 for the use of the Dean and Chapter of
Westminster.'

A man determined to use his will to vent a lifetime of
vexation against his wife was farmer Thomas Benjamin
Adcock of Surrey who died in 1774 and wrote:

'Whereas it was my misfortune to be made very uneasy
by ——, my wife, for many years from our marriage, by
her turbulent behaviour, for she was not content to
despise my admonitions, but she contrived every method
to make me unhappy; she was so perverse in her nature

that she would not be reclaimed, but seemed only to be born to be a plague to me; the strength of Samson, the knowledge of Homer, the prudence of Augustus, the cunning of Pyrrhus, the patience of Job, the subtlety of Hannibal and the watchfulness of Hermogenes could not have been sufficient to subdue her; for no skill or force in the world would make her good; and as we have lived separate and apart from each other for eight years, and, she having perverted her son to leave and totally abandon me, therefore, I give her a shilling.'

Some sly digs at the characters of a number of his friends and enemies characterised the will of Edward Wortley Montague who died in Padua in 1776. He wrote:

'To the Earl of . . . , I do not give any part of my property because of the best part of that he has contrived to take already.

'To Sir Francis . . . , I give one word of mine, because he has never had the good fortune to keep his own.

'To Lord M. . . , I give nothing, because I know he'll bestow it on the poor.

'To Sir Robert W. . . . , I leave my political opinions, never doubting he can well turn them into cash, who has always found such an excellent market in which to change his own.

'To Sir Leopold D. . . , I give my cast-off habit of swearing oaths, in consideration that no oaths have ever been able to find him yet.'

Although snuff-taking was a popular practice in eighteenth-century England, few people can have gone to the lengths of a very curious old lady named Margaret Thompson of Westminster, London, who was obviously addicted to the drug and requested in her will of 1777:

'*Item.* That on my decease my coffin is to be filled with Scotch snuff until it completely covers my body.
'*Item.* The bearers of my coffin are to be six snuff takers from the parish of St James's Westminster.
'*Item.* That the clergyman who conducts the service will walk in front of the coffin, taking snuff as he progresses.
'*Item.* That my faithful servant, M . . . will go ahead of the procession and scattering snuff along the ground as well as among those who look on.'

So incensed was the unknown recipient of the 'bequest' in the following will made by John Hylett Stow in 1781 that he took out a suit for libel and successfully obtained

considerable damages for defamation from the dead man's estate: a factor which undoubtedly gave him the last laugh on his malicious benefactor.

'I hereby direct my executors to lay out five guineas in the purchase of a picture of the viper biting the benevolent hand of the person who saved him from perishing in the snow, if the same can be bought for the money; and that they do, in memory of me, present it to ——, Esq., a king's counsel, whereby he may have frequent opportunities of contemplating it, and, by a comparison between that and his own virtue, be able to form a certain judgement which is best and most profitable, a grateful remembrance of past friendship and almost parental regard, or ingratitude and insolence. This I direct to be presented to him in lieu of a legacy of three thousand pounds I had by a former will, now revoked and burned, left him.'

William Shackwell, who was a city official in Plymouth, Devon, for many years, was anxious to ensure that he was not buried alive, as well as passing on some good advice to his wife – as he demonstrated in his will of October 1782:

'I desire that my body may be kept as long as it may not be offensive, and that one of my toes or fingers may be

cut off to secure a certainty of my being dead.

'I also make this further request to my dear wife. That as she has been troubled with one old fool, she will not think of marrying a second.'

By a strange twist of fate an Englishman named Thomas Williamson who nursed a deep-seated hatred of the Irish was bequeathed a large piece of property in Tipperary – but only on the condition he lived on the land. Grudgingly accepting the condition, Williamson nevertheless managed to cause equal surprise among his relatives when his own will was opened on 17 March, 1791 to disclose the following instructions:

'I give and bequeath the annual sum of ten pounds, to be paid in perpetuity out of my estate, to the following purpose. It is my will and pleasure that this sum shall be spent in the purchase of a certain quantity of the liquor vulgarly called whisky, and it shall be publicly given out that a certain number of persons, Irish only, not to exceed twenty, who may choose to assemble in the cemetery in which I shall be interred, on the anniversary of my death, shall have the same distributed to them. Further, it is my desire that each shall receive it by half-a-pint at a time till the whole is consumed, each being likewise provided with a stout oaken stick and a knife, and that they shall drink it all on the spot. Knowing what I know of the Irish character, my conviction is, that with these materials given, they will not fail to destroy each other, and when in the course of time the race comes to be exterminated, this neighbourhood at least may, perhaps, be colonised by civilised and respectable Englishmen.'

A father anxious to reproach a wayward son took a most unusual – not to mention gruesome – means of doing so in his will of January 1793. Philip Thicknesse of London wrote:

'I leave my right hand, to be cut off after my death, to my son Lord Audley, and I desire it may be sent to him, in hopes that such a sight might remind him of his duty to God, after having so long abandoned the duty he owed to a father who once loved him so affectionately.'

The Countess of Loudoun also made this gruesome and rather mysterious request in her will in 1798:

'After my death I direct my right hand to be cut off,

and buried in Donnington Park, at the bend of the hill toward the Trent, with this motto over it: "I byde my tyme".'

A member of the landed gentry, John Withipol of Walthamstow, near London, left all his property and estate to his wife, declaring in his will of 1798:

'Trusting – yea, I may say, as I think, assuring myself that she will marry no man, for fear to meet with so evil a husband as I have been to her.'

Before going to sea in 1804, Scottish seaman Duncan Forbes drew up his will in Aberdeen and requested his executor:

'In the event of my decease, to pay my wife one shilling, that she might buy hazelnuts, as she has always preferred cracking nuts to mending my clothes.'

The codicil which Lord Nelson wrote to his will as he lay dying on his flagship, *Victory*, at the battle of Trafalgar on

the morning of 21 October, 1805, may well have been intended to be humorous – particularly in view of the passionate nature which the lady in question, his mistress, was reputed to possess:

'I leave Emma Lady Hamilton, therefore, a Legacy to my King and Country.'

In the curious will of John Tuke of Wath, near Rotherham, England, who died in 1810, the old man bequeathed:

'1 shilling to every poor woman in Wath; 10s 6d, to the ringers to ring a peal of grandbobs, which are to strike off while I am being put in my grave; forty dozen penny loaves to be thrown down from the church leads on Christmas Day forever. Also £1 1s per annum to the old woman who has for eleven years tucked me up in bed; and one penny to every child that attends my funeral.'

(According to local tradition, between 600 and 700 children turned up to claim their penny!)

From the will of a London merchant, James Porter, who left legacies to all his servants *except* his steward. He declared of this man in 1811:

'Having been in my service in that capacity twenty years, I have too high an opinion of his shrewdness to suppose he has not already sufficiently enriched himself.'

A hard-living, extrovert English gentleman, Daniel Martinett, who died in Calcutta, India, made the following amusing remarks in signing off his will in 1825:

'As to this fulsome carcase of mine, having already seen enough of worldly pomp, I desire nothing relative to it to be done, only its being stowed away in my old green chest, to avoid expense for as I lived profusely, I die frugally.

'The undertaker's fees will come to nothing, as I won them from him at a game of billiards, in the presence of Mr Thomas Morrice and William Perkes, at the said William Perkes' house, in February last.

'I furthermore request that the Reverend Mr Henry Butler read the prayers which are customary at burials, and also preach a sermon on Sunday next after my decease, taking his text from Solomon, "All is vanity". In consideration of which, over and above his fees, I

bestow upon him all my hypocrisy, which he wants as a modern good man; but as my finances are low, and cannot conveniently discharge his fees, I hope he will please accept the will for the deed.'

A hole in the pier head at Dover, England, led to a very strange bequest to the town from Mr Henry Matson. As a result of losing a favourite gold-headed walking stick through this hole into the sea, he stated in his will of 1826:

'I direct that the sum below mentioned shall be left to the Corporation of Dover, and the interest accruing therefrom each year shall be used to stop up all such holes on the pierhead.
'After this work has been carried out, any surplus is to be used for the refreshment of the Officers of the Corporation.'

An eccentric London doctor, Thomas Ellerby, left explicit instructions about the disposal of his corpse – and a dire threat if his wishes were not carried out, as his will of February 1827 reveals:

'*Item.* I desire that immediately after my death my body

shall be carried to the Anatomical Museum in Aldersgate
Street, and shall be there dissected by Drs Lawrence,
Tyrell, and Wardrop.

'*Item.* I bequeath my heart to Mr W., anatomist; my
lungs to Mr R., and my brains to Mr F., in order that
they may preserve them from decomposition.

'And I declare that if these gentlemen shall fail
faithfully to execute these my last wishes in this respect I
will come – if it should be by any means possible – and
torment them until they shall comply.'

An extraordinary French Justice of the Peace, M. Hellion,
who lived near Caen in Normandy, spent almost his entire
life reclining on a couch or lying in bed. This in no way
affected his work, however, and he conducted many of his
duties as a magistrate in his bedroom. Vivid impressions
remained of him long after his death, lying outstretched
with his head on a pillow while cases were argued before
him. When he died in June 1828, his will proved to be as
eccentric as his life had been:

'I decree that I should be buried at night, in bed, and in
the position in which death catches me – viz., with my
mattress, sheets, blankets, pillows – and, in short, all that
constitutes the belongings of a bedstead.'

(*In accordance with these wishes, a huge pit was dug, M.*

Mellion and his bed lowered into it, and boards overlaid so that this tranquillity could continue undisturbed even after death!)

Paul Sebastian, an eccentric minister of St Ives in Cornwall who evidently had a penchant for gambling – or else a very perverse sense of humour – bequeathed a sum of money to his chapel with these words in his will of 1829:

'That the money provide six Bibles every year, for which six men and six women are to throw dice on Whit Tuesday after the morning service, the minister kneeling the while at the south end of the Communion table, and praying to God to direct the luck to His glory.'

Another eccentric member of the clergy, the Reverend Luke Imber of Christchurch, Dorset, who at the age of 83 married a country girl of 13, decreed in his will of 1832:

'That I be buried in an old chest which I have for some time kept for this purpose, and that the bearers shall have a pair of tanned leather gloves and a new pair of shoes to carry out this purpose.'

What seemed at first sight like a generous bequest to a wife had a sting in its tail in this will made in May 1833 by John Caldecott of Walworth, London:

'I leave my widow the sum of five hundred pounds. But she is only to come into the enjoyment of it after her death – in order that she may be buried suitably as my widow.'

An Hungarian opera lover, Stanislas Polzmarz, decided to try to encourage a rather bashful young friend named Lotz, whom he believed could be a fine opera singer, to perform publicly, and to this end inserted the following curious clause in his will made in 1835:

'I hereby bequeath the sum of three million florins to the aforementioned Lotz on the condition that before claiming it he shall engage himself at the Scala Theatre in Milan to perform in the operas of *Othello* and *La Sonnambula*. Having heard him, at an evening party, sing fragments of the parts of Elvino and Othello, and admired the beauty of his tenor, I believe he can become a favourite of the whole musical world.

'If, therefore, I am right, he will thank me, and so will all *dilettenti, for* my acumen; if, on the other hand, he should fail, he will have money enough to compensate for the hisses he may incur.'

2
VICTORIAN
LEGACIES

One of the very first wills published after Queen Victoria came to the throne was that of a typically strict parent leaving a considerable inheritance to his only daughter – but with the severest penalty if she did not follow his curious rules about female modesty. The Reverend Ebenezer Potts, the rector of Whitby in Yorkshire, addressed himself thus to his daughter, Anna, in his will of 1837:

'Seeing that my daughter Anna has not availed herself of my advice touching the objectionable practice of going about with her arms bare up to the elbows, my will is that, should she continue after my death in this violation of the modesty of her sex, all the goods, chattels, moneys, land and other property that I have devised to her for the maintenance of her future life shall pass to the oldest of the sons of my sister, Caroline. Should anyone take exception to this my wish as being too severe, I answer that licence in dress in a woman is a mark of a depraved mind.'

Despite his enormous wealth, Richard Watson, of Surrey, felt miserly towards at least one of his servants, instructing his executors in his will of 1838:

'To ensure that the night shirt in which I am laid out be not a new one but an old one – as it will become the perquisite of the nurse.'

In order to frustrate the designs of undertakers whom she believed charged extortionate rates for their services, the Dowager Countess of Sandwich declared in her will of 1838:

'I therefore forbid all grotesque paraphernalia, desiring only to be buried quietly and decently, with no scarfs, hatbands, or other excuses for fraud and cheating.'

Obviously wishing to see that he was properly mourned, James Robins of Newcastle declared in his will of 1840:

'I bequeath to my wife the sum of £30, but with the particular request that she should wear widow's dress. If she should fail to comply with this term, I instruct that the sum should be reduced to £20.'

André Leroux, a successful gambler and card-player, left his fortune to his friends in Toulouse with these instructions in his will, dated 1846:

'My sole condition on those to whom I give this sum is that they should place a deck of cards inside the coffin beside my body, thereafter carrying me to the grave, and on the way stopping to drink a glass of wine at the saloon where we passed so many agreeable evenings at piquet.'

An obviously humorous man named Clegg who described himself as a 'conjuror' by profession, left the following amusing instructions for his funeral in a will published in 1846. He prefaced his remarks with the comment that his wishes were only to be carried out 'if I should die a natural death within two miles of Shaw Chapel, or escape hanging'.

'I desire that my executors should assemble three score of the truest of my friends – not to include any woman, nor yet any man whose avocations compel him to wear a white cap or apron, nor any man in the habit of taking snuff or using tobacco. Four fiddlers are to attend, and the company are to make merry and dance. For the refreshment of those assembled they are to be provided

with sixty-two spiced buns and twenty shillings' worth of
the best ale.

'My body, dressed in roast-meat (or best) clothes, is to
be laid on a bier in the midst of this assembly. All are to
make merry for two hours, after which the cortege may
proceed to the graveyard led by the curate riding upon an
ass, for which service he is to receive a fee of one guinea.
No one may weep and all should repair to the public
house where I was best-known and there eat and drink
as they please to the amount of thirty shillings.'

The will of the eccentric and extremely wealthy French
nobleman, the Marquis D'Aligre, made in 1847, contained
a number of amusing bequests, including one of 20,000
francs to a faithful retainer to take care of his four pet rats!
Among the others were:

'I leave 200,000 francs a year to the "Phalansteinans",
but they are only to receive this sum on the day in which
they shall have transformed the ocean into orangeade,
and gratified mankind with that appendage he needs to
make him equal to the gibbon.

'To Mme N. . . . , who was full of attention for me, I
leave one broken cup. And I declare that all the while
she thought she was taking me in, I was laughing in my
sleeve at the grimace she would make when she

discovered it was I who had got all her little gifts – her smiles and favours – and had no intention of repaying them as she expected.

'I withdraw from M. A. . . . and M.V. . . . the sums I had left them by a former will; they have so often proclaimed that I am a man who would cut a farthing in four, that I would on no account oblige them to change their opinion.

'Finally, I leave to my relatives, oblivion; to my friends, ingratitude; to God, my soul. As for my body, it belongs to my family vault.'

William Kinsett of London expressed the desire in his will of October 1855, that his body should be burned after his death. As this request predates the now commonplace practice of cremation, his instructions make interesting, not to say ultimately amusing, reading:

'Believing in the impolicy of interring the dead amidst the living, and as an example to others, I give my body, four days after death, to the directors of the Imperial Gas Company, London, to be placed in one of their retorts and consumed to ashes, and that they be paid ten pounds by my executors for the trouble this act will impose upon them for so doing. Should a defence of fanaticism and superstition prevent their granting this my request, then my executors must submit

to have my remains buried, in the plainest manner
possible, in my family grave in St John's Wood
Cemetery, to assist in poisoning the living in that
neighbourhood.'

Peter Labelliere of Sussex also reached the end of his days
with a wry sense of humour about life, and gave these
instructions in his will of June 1860:

'I desire to be buried head downwards, because the
world is topsy-turvy, and it is fit that I be so buried that
I might be right at last.'

A wealthy London landowner with an abhorrence of
moustaches gave a solemn warning as to the consequences
of his sons wearing them in his will of 1862:

'In case my son Edward shall wear moustaches, then
the devise hereinbefore contained in favour of him,
his appointees, heirs, and assigns of my said estate
called Pepper Park, Twickenham, shall be void; and I
devise the same estate to my son William, his
appointees, heirs and assigns. And in case my said son
William shall wear moustaches, then the devise
hereinbefore contained in favour of him, his appointees,

heirs and assigns of my said estate called Pepper Park, Twickenham, shall be void; and I devise the said estate to my said son, Edward, his appointees, heirs, and assigns.'

Another man who shared the same view was an upholsterer in Pimlico named Fleming who left bequests to each of his employees in his will of 1869 thus:

'I hereby bequeath £10 to each man in my employ that does not wear a moustache. To those who persist in wearing them £5 only.'

Farmer Thomas Hollis of Cuiscombe, Dorset, proved himself a modest, unpretentious man when he declared in his will of 1869:

'That my corpse be buried in one of my cornfields, ten feet below the surface, and the ground to be immediately ploughed, so that no trace of the spot remains.'

A lady with a similar desire to have as little fuss as possible made over her body was Lady Truro who died at her home at Shooter's Hill, London, in 1869:

'I desire that my body be buried by my husband in a shallow grave on the lawn fronting the house, at a spot which I have already selected. Furthermore that I am laid in a lightly constructed box so that the process of decay may not be arrested.'

Very bizarre instructions for the use of his body – his skin in particular – were given by Stanley Sanbom of Medford, Massachusetts, in his will of 1871. Bequeathing his corpse to the Museum of Anatomy at Harvard University, he went on:

'I further request that, after the example of John Ziska, my skin should be converted into two drumheads, not for the same purpose as that intimated by the Bohemian chief for the frightening of his enemies, but to become the property of my distinguished friend and patriotic fellow citizen, Warren Simpson, drummer of Cohapel, on condition that he will, on the 17th June every year at sunrise, beat on the said drum the tune of "Yankee Doodle" on Bunker's Hill. The drumheads to be respectively inscribed with Pope's "Universal Prayer" and the Declaration of Independence, as originally worded by its illustrious author, Thomas Jefferson.
'The remainder of my body useless for anatomical purposes, to be composted for a fertiliser to contribute to

the growth of an American Elm, to be planted in some rural thoroughfare, that the weary wayfarer may rest, and innocent children may play, beneath its umbrageous branches rendered luxuriant by my remains.'

A passionate temperance fighter and fitness fanatic, James Sargeant of Leicester, in England, bequeathed his estate to his two idle and dissipated nephews, but only on the following stringent conditions laid down in his will of 1871:

'As my nephews are fond of indulging themselves in bed in the morning, and as I wish them to prove to the satisfaction of my executors that they have got out of bed in the morning, and either employed themselves in business or taken exercise in the open air, from five to eight o'clock every morning from the fifth of April to the 10th of October, being three hours every day, and from seven to nine o'clock in the morning from the 10th of October to the 5th of April, being two hours every morning; this is to be done for some years, during the first seven years to the satisfaction of my executors, who may excuse them in case of illness, but the task must be made up when they are well, and if they will not do this, they shall not receive any share of my property. Temperance makes the faculties clear, and exercise

makes them vigorous. It is temperance and exercise that can alone ensure the fittest state for mental or bodily exertion.'

In a bizarre will published in Alton, Hampshire, in 1874, a citizen named John Furstone left his fortune to anyone capable of fulfilling these conditions:

'Having no family of my own, I leave the sum of £7,000 to any man legitimately bearing the name of Furstone who should discover and marry a female also bearing the name Furstone.
'If the marriage should result in children, what money remains should descend to the male off-spring, if any; or else to any child or children of the opposite sex who should, after marriage, retain the name Furstone.'

The crafty nature of a certain Major Hook of Ham Common in London, enabled him to keep in operation a bequest to his wife long after it should have ceased. Mrs Hook had been the recipient of an annuity bequeathed to her in these words:

'And the sum herebefore mentioned shall be paid to the said Sarah Jane Hook as long as she is above ground.'

(On her death in 1874, the Major decided to take advantage of the somewhat ambiguous terms and ensure she stayed above ground. To this end he had her body placed in a coffin in a room of his home covered by a glass case. 'For thirty years,' says a contemporary report, 'he thus prolonged his enjoyment, if not of his wife's society, at least of her income!')

A man of high ideals but limited resources to carry them out was an eccentric Bristol clergyman, the Reverend William Hill, who died in November 1875, leaving his estate of £3,000 towards the destruction of the British Empire and the prevention of drinking. He wrote in his will:

'I pray for the king of Zion to overthrow the politico-ecclesiastical establishment of the British Empire, and I leave the world with a full conviction that such prayer must ere long be answered.

'I likewise declare that the drinking customs of professors and non-professors are doomed, and trust that Heaven will dash this work of the Devil from earth.'

An unhappy husband named Thomas Darley of Manchester, who suffered mightily from his wife's light fingers, declared in his will of 1876:

'To my wife, Eliza, I leave one shilling for she has picked my pocket of sixty guineas.'

Another husband who found the words to express his displeasure towards his wife but could not deprive her of at least a small portion of his estate was a London bookseller, Edward Parker, who wrote in 1875:

'I bequeath the sum of £50 to Elizabeth whom, through my foolish fondness, I made my wife, without regard to family, fame or fortune; and who, in return, has not spared, most unjustly, to accuse me of every crime regarding human nature, save highway robbery.'

A Parisian eccentric, Monsieur Benôit, of the rue des Gravillers, filed these instructions with the notary of the French capital in his will of October 1877:

'I expressly and formally desire that my remains may be enclosed for burial in my large leather trunk, instead of

putting my survivors to the expense of a coffin. I am attached to that trunk, which has gone round the world with me three times.'

Old watches have been popular legacies for generations, but there can have been few stranger bequests than that of Peter MacAndrews of Glasgow to his son in January 1877:

'I bequeath my two worst watches to my son, because I know he is sure to dissect them.'

Being worth their weight in gold was made literally true in the case of two Scottish girls whose father – turning upside down the idea that all his race are mean – made this provision in his will in 1877. Thomas Black of Kilmarnock declared:

'And as for my daughters, M . . . and J. . . , I direct that my executor should have them weighed, and then give to each the equivalent weight in one pound bank notes.'

(The younger girl, who was somewhat plump, did better than her older sister, receiving £57,344 from the will, while the other got a mere £51,200!)

Walter Brunberger, a renowned Berlin drinker, made two special requests in his will filed in 1879:

'First, that the sum of ten thousand marks be set in a fund so that the interest therefrom may weekly provide a quarter of a tun of Bavarian beer for my friends in the Prinzenstrasse, this to continue as long as these contemporaries shall survive.

'Secondly, that my friends will take it in turns to roll a barrel of beer behind my hearse to the cemetery, and thereafter consume it upon my grave.'

A Yorkshire mill-owner named Thomas Keighley who had a large family and a great many relatives decided on this novel way of dividing his estate, according to his will made in 1879:

'I therefore declare that my executor is empowered to divide my properties among only those of my descendants who are permanently resident in the said county of Yorkshire and also measure not less than six feet four inches in height.'

An elderly Canadian, Doctor Dunlop, of Winnipeg,
Canada, made some stinging remarks on the characters of
his various beneficiaries in his will published in 1879:

'To my eldest sister Joan, my five-acre field, to console
her for being married to a man she is obliged to henpeck.

'To my second sister Sally, the cottage that stands
beyond the said field with its garden, because as no one is
likely to marry her it will be large enough to lodge her.

'To my third sister Kate, the family Bible,
recommending her to learn as much of its spirit as she
already knows of its letter, that she may become a better
Christian.

'To my fourth sister Mary, my grandmother's silver
snuff-box, that she may not be ashamed to take snuff
before company.

'To my fifth sister, Lydia, my silver drinking-cup for
reasons known to herself.

'To my brother Ben, my books, that he may learn to
read with them.

'To my brother James, my big silver watch, that he can
know the hour at which men ought to rise from their
beds.

'To my brother-in-law Jack, a punch bowl, because he
will do credit to it.

'To my brother-in-law Christopher, my best pipe, out
of gratitude that he married my sister Maggie whom no
man of taste would have taken.

'To my friend John Caddell, a silver teapot, that, being afflicted with a slatternly wife, he may therefrom drink to his comfort.

'To George Caddell, my friend's son, a silver tankard, which I would fain leave to old John himself lest he should commit the sacrilege of melting it down to make temperance medals.'

A peculiar American will which produced a most surprising outcome was filed in New York in 1880. The last testament of John Stewart Hale declared:

'I bequeath all my fortune to my nephews and nieces, seven in number. They are to share it equally, and on no account to go to law about it, on pain of forfeiting their respective shares.

'I own seventy-one pairs of trousers, and I strictly enjoin my executors to hold a public sale at which these shall be sold to the highest bidder, and the proceeds distributed to the poor of the city.

'I desire that these garments shall in no way be examined or meddled with, but be disposed of as they are found at the time of my death; and no purchaser is to buy more than one pair.'

(The executors faithfully carried out Mr Hale's wishes and the

*trousers were sold to seventy-one different purchasers. One can
imagine the surprise and delight of these people when, on
examining the trousers, a small packet was found sewn to a
pocket in every pair containing bank notes to the value of
$1,000! The heirs to the estate were, of course, doubly
frustrated by Hale's will from taking any action to dispute it for
he had expressly forbidden them to examine the trousers or go to
law without forfeiting their bequests!)*

There can surely have been few wills less likely to get a
claim lodged on them than that filed by the curiously
named Mr Smith Willie of Pennsylvania in 1880. He even
went to the extraordinary length of requiring his executors
to appoint a 'jury of honour' to examine any possible
claims consisting of 'all the householders in my native
town who can prove they came honestly by their fortunes'.
The will itself read:

'Seeing that I have no direct descendants, and that I am
wholly unacquainted with those I may possess
collaterally, I bequeath my fortune to any one among
them who, in the course of the twelve-month from the
date of my death, may distinguish himself by an act of
heroism worthy of ancient times.
'In case none of my collateral descendants should be
justified in making this claim, I then leave all I possess to
be divided between all the women who can prove that

they have been my mistresses, be it for ever so brief a period.'

A doctor with little regard for his own corpse gave these perfunctory instructions for its disposal after his death. Writing his will in 1883, Dr Messenger Mouncey of Chelsea Hospital said:

'I bequeath my body for dissection, and after the surgeons have completed their task, they may put what remains into a deal box in which holes have been made, and throw it into the River Thames.'

A man who prided himself on his sense of humour, Walter Allen of Kent, made a will in 1884 full of the most appalling puns, of which these instructions for the mode of his burial can be taken as typical:

'The coffin is to be of red fir. I pine for nothing better. Even this may be thought a deal too good, though certainly not very spruce . . .'

A Washington DC financier, Osbert Wells, made this double-edged proviso to his daughter in his will filed in 1887:

'Should my daughter marry and be afflicted with children, the trustees are to pay out of said legacy, Ten Thousand Dollars on the birth of the first child to the Washington General Hospital; Twenty Thousand Dollars on the second; Thirty Thousand Dollars on the third; and an additional Ten Thousand Dollars on the birth of each fresh child till the One Hundred and Fifty Thousand Dollars is exhausted. Should any portion of this sum be left at the end of twenty years, the balance is to be paid to her to use as she thinks fit.'

An American theatre attendant, John Reed, who silently nursed an ambition to appear on the stage of the Walnut Tree Theatre in Philadelphia where he worked for forty-four years, achieved his life-long desire by this peculiar request in his will of 1887:

'My head to be separated from my body immediately after my death; the latter to be buried in a grave; the former, duly macerated and prepared, to be brought to the theatre, where I have served all my life, and to be

employed to represent the skull of Yorick – and to this
end I bequeath my head to the properties.'

The Reverend Langton Freeman, rector of Bilton,
Northamptonshire, had a horror of burial and requested a
special resting place for his corpse in his will of 1888:

'*Item.* My body shall be left undisturbed on the bed
whereon I die and there remain until it can no longer
be kept. Then it is to be carried, bed and all, decently
and privately, to the summer house in my garden at
Whitton. The bed and body are to be wrapped in a
strong double-winding sheet and treated in all respect
as was the body of Our Lord. The doors and windows
of the summer house are to be secured and the
building planted round with evergreen and fenced with
dark blue palings.'

A French lawyer, Jacques Pascal of Colmar, a man with a
sense of humour and possibly something of a guilty
conscience – bequeathed his fortune of 100,000 francs to a
local institution with these words in 1888:

'I have acquired this money among those who spend

their lives in litigation. It is, then, only a restitution and so I give it to the hospital for lunatics.'

A rich Polish landlord, M. Zalesky, left property in Warsaw valued at 100,000 roubles and a will which proved frustrating in the extreme. The document was enclosed in an envelope bearing the words 'To be opened on my death' which was duly performed in 1889.

Inside was another envelope which read: 'To be opened six weeks after my death.'

When this period had passed and the second envelope was opened, a third was revealed bearing the words: 'To be opened one year after my death.'

This same procedure was, in fact, continued several more times until the year 1894 when the old man's heirs, having become increasingly annoyed at each envelope, at last came upon the actual will itself. It proved to be just as eccentric as the directions which had preceded its opening:

'I bequeath half of my fortune to such of my heirs, heretofore mentioned, as has the largest number of children.

'And I direct that the rest of my property be placed in a bank, and a hundred years from the date of my death, this is to be divided, with the accumulated interest, among my descendants.'

John B. Luther, a wealthy American bachelor from Fall River, Massachusetts, who left a fortune valued at over 100,000 dollars, teasingly forestalled the claims he expected to be made on his estate with these words in his will filed in San Francisco in 1890:

'I do hereby declare that I am not married and that I have no children. I have noticed, however, the facility with which sworn testimony can be procured and produced in support of the claims of alleged widows and adopted children, and the frequent recurrence of such claims in recent years. I therefore make express provision in this my last will as follows: I give and bequeath to such person as shall be found, proved, and established to be my surviving wife or widow, whether the marriage be found to have taken place before or after the execution of this will, the sum of $5, and to each and every person who shall be found, proved, and established to be my child by birth, adoption, acknowledgement, or otherwise, and whether before or after the execution of this will, the sum of $5, and I declare that I do intentionally omit to make for any of the persons in this paragraph referred to any other or further provision.'

Miss Jessica Carr, a reclusive New York spinster who only ventured out from her home to visit church once a week, made this peculiar bequest and condition in her will of 1893:

'I desire that all my estate be realised and the money employed in the building of a new church in my neighbourbood, my one stipulation being that my remains, after decent attentions, should be mixed up in the mortar used for the laying of the first stone.'

Piet Klaes, a wealthy linen merchant who was also widely known in Holland as 'The King of Smokers' and had erected a large house near Rotterdam which he filled with an enormous collection of pipes from all over the world, naturally enough reflected this life-long interest in his will published in 1893:

'It is my wish to be buried in an oaken coffin lined with the cedar from my old Havana cigar boxes, and a box of French caporal and a packet of old Dutch tobacco placed at my feet. My favourite pipe is to be by my side, along with a box of matches, a flint and steel, and some tinder, as there is no knowing what may happen where I am going.

'I further desire that all the smokers of the country should be invited to my funeral, that each should be

presented with 10 lb of tobacco and two Dutch pipes of
the newest fashion, on which should be engraved my
name, arms and the date of my decease.

'Lastly I request that all my relatives, friends and
funeral guests be careful to keep their pipes alight during
the funeral ceremonies, after which they should empty
the ashes from their pipes on my coffin.'

Broken-hearted lovers have written many bizarre last
testaments before attempting, successfully or
unsuccessfully, to commit suicide. Perhaps the strangest of
all such wills was made by an unknown London man in
1894 and published a few years later by Dr Forbes Winslow
of the Royal College of Surgeons who swore that it had
been 'literally carried out':

'Having been crossed in love and determined to end an
unhappy life, I desire that my body shall be boiled down
and all the fat extracted therefrom. This fat is to be used
in making a candle which is then to be presented to D . . . ,
the object of my affections, together with a letter
enclosed containing my farewells and expressions of
undying love.

'I further desire that the candle and letter should be
delivered at night, in order that my beloved might read
these lines by the light of my dying love.'

William Vanderbilt, a relative of the famous American financier and railroad magnate, Cornelius Vanderbilt, gave one of the strangest reasons for a personal bequest in his will filed in 1896:

'I supplicate Miss B . . . to accept my whole fortune, too feeble an acknowledgement of the inexpressible sensation which the contemplation of her adorable nose has produced on me.'

An eccentric French nobleman who delighted in conundrums decided to settle his quite considerable estate on his six nieces and nephews. However, the will of the Marquis de Renaud, filed in 1896, listed the following conditions which had to be satisfied before the young relatives came into their money:

'Every one of my nephews must marry a woman named Antonie, and every one of my nieces marry a man called Anton.
'I require that they must all celebrate their marriages on one of the St Anthony's Days, either 17 January, 10 May or 13 June.
'And I further require that they give the Christian name Antonie or Anton to every first-born child according to sex.

'If any of these conditions are not fulfilled then my bequests are void.'

William Farren, a Cambridge man with an evident grudge against the students of the town's famous university, made this declaration in his will published in 1900:

'I fervently hope that by the disposition of my property that my family are saved from keeping or living in an undergraduate lodging-house, as undergraduates are more like wolves and dogs than human beings.'

An aged German professor named Weindorf, seemingly intent on preventing his only living relative from long enjoying his estate, inserted the following bizarre clause in his will made in Berlin in 1900:

'I therefore leave all my property to Herr . . . , but on the absolute condition that he should wear white linen clothes at all seasons of the year, and must on no account supplement them in winter by extra undergarments.'

A London playboy and music-hall lover, Thomas Blyth of Kensington, who died in 1900, left a surprisingly large fortune, but expressly forbade anyone to whom he bequeathed money to wear mourning for him – or else they would forfeit their inheritances. He did, though, make one exception:

'But I cannot forget the kindness of the ladies who have promised to wear Dolly Varden garters of black and white as a mark of respect for my memory.'

A love-lorn Cincinnati phrenologist and physician Professor Byrd Powell, who fell deeply in love with one of his married lady pupils, a Mrs Kinsey, offered her a most grisly token of his affection in order that she might remember him as well as continuing her studies, in his will of 1901:

'I do bequeath to her whom I have so admired, my head and my heart, these to be taken from my body by Mr H. T. Kekeler and given to her for her use.'

Virgil Harris, an American lawyer and collector of old wills, came across the last testament of an old Victorian

bachelor made in 1901, in which the man asked for his property to be divided equally between three ladies.

'I declare that my wealth such as it is found to be, should be shared between the three ladies undermentioned, to whom I proposed marriage and each of whom refused me. The reason for my bequest, should any of these ladies enquire it, is that by their refusal I owe them all my earthly happiness.'

3
TESTAMENTARY
VERSES

Despite the fact that the making of a will is considered a serious business, quite a number of people have chosen to make their last testaments in verse – the earliest of these being William Hunnis, an apparently sober gentleman who served for much of his life as the Chapel Master to Queen Elizabeth I. For the first time in his life he felt the urge to resort to poetry to express his final wishes: and in so doing began a tradition which has remained acceptable in the eyes of the law to this day. Hunnis' will made about 1580 declared:

> To God my soule I do bequeathe, because it is his own,
> My body to be layd in grave, where to my friends best
>   knowen;
> Executors I will none make, thereby great stryfe may
>   grow,
> Because the goods that I shall leave wyll not pay all I
>   owe.

A Wiltshire carpenter, David Prosser, was moved to versify when it came to making his will in 1690 – and similarly showed himself a man of humour:

> In the name of God, Amen:
> My featherbed to my wife, Jen;
> Also my carpenter's saw and hammer;
> Until she marries; then, God damn her!

John Hedges of Finchley in Middlesex got quite carried away when he composed his will in verse in July 1737:

> This fifth of May
> Being airy and gay,
> To trip not inclined,
> But of vigorous mind,
> And my body in health,
> I'll dispose of my wealth;
> And of all I'm to leave
> On this side of the grave,
> To some one or other,
> I think to my brother.
>
> But because I presaw
> That my brother-in-law
> I did not take care,
> Would come in for a share,
> Which I noways intended,
> Till their manners were mended –
> And of that there's no sign.
>
> I do therefore enjoin,
> And strictly command,
> As witness my hand,
> That nought I have got
> To be brought to hotch-pot.

And I give and devise,
Much as in me lies,
To the son of my mother,
My own dear brother,
To have and to hold
All my silver and gold,
As the affectionate pledges
Of his brother,

John Hedges

A Yorkshireman, William Hickington, was similarly
taken by the muse and his will of 1770 was accepted by the
Deanery Court of York in that same year:

This is my last will,
I insist on it still;
To sneer on and welcome,
And e'en laugh your fill.
I, William Hickington,
Poet of Pocklington,
Do give and bequeath,
As free as I breathe,
To thee, Mary Jarum,
The Queen of my Harum,
My cash and my cattle,
With every chattel,

To have and to hold,
Come heat or come cold,
Sans hindrance or strife,
Though thou art not my wife.
As witness my hand,
Just here as I stand,
The twelfth of July,
In the year Seventy.

The earliest humorous will in verse written by a woman was the following example filed by Monica Swiney of Dulwich, London in 1776:

Of this I never will repent,
'Tis my last Will and testament,
If much or little – nay, my all –
I give my brother, Matthew Gall;
And this will hinder any bother,
My sister Strich or Mic, our brother:
Yet stop! should Mat die before Mic,
And that may happen for Death's quick,
I then bequeath my worldly store
To brother Mic for evermore;

But should I outlive my brothers,
It's fit that then I think of others.

Matthew has sons, and daughters, too,
'Tis all their own, were it Peru.
Pray, Mr Forrest, don't sit still,
But witness this as my last Will.

Another Londoner, Will Jackett of Islington, penned
these light-hearted lines in July 1789:

I give and bequeath,
When I'm laid underneath,
To my two loving sisters most dear,
The whole of my store,
Were it twice as much more,
Which God's goodness has given me here.

And that none may prevent
This my will and intent,
Or occasion the least of law-racket,
With a solemn appeal
I confirm, sign, and seal
This the true act and deed of Will Jackett.

Surely one of the most delightful and amusing wills in verse
is this example written by gentleman farmer William Luffell
of Shimpling in Suffolk which he made in March 1803:

As this life must soon end, and my frame will decay,
And my soul to some far-distant clime wing its way,
Ere that time arrives, now I free am from cares,
I thus wish to settle my worldly affairs,
A course right and proper men of sense will agree.
I am now strong and hearty, my age forty-three;
I make this my last will, as I think 'tis quite time,
It conveys all I wish, though 'tis written in rhyme.
To employ an attorney I ne'er was inclin'd,
They are pests to society, sharks of mankind.
To avoid that base tribe my own will I now draw,
May I ever escape coming under their paw.
To Ezra Dalton, my nephew, I give all my land,
With the old Gothic cottage that thereon doth stand;
'Tis near Shimpling great road, in which I now dwell,
It looks like a chapel or hermit's old cell,
Urlth my furniture, plate and linen likewise,
And securities, money, with what may arise.
'Tis my wish and desire that he should enjoy these,
And pray let him take even my skin, if he please.
To my loving, kind sister I give and bequeath,
For her tender regard, when this world I shall leave,
If she choose to accept it, my rump-bone may take,
And tip it with silver, a whistle to make.
My brother-in-law is a strange-tempered dog;
He's as fierce as a tiger, in manners a hog;
A petty tyrant at home, his frowns how they dread;
Two ideas at once never entered his head.

So proud and so covetous, moreover so mean,
I dislike to look at him, the fellow is so lean.
He ne'er behaved well, and, though very unwilling,
Yet I feel that I must cut him off with a shilling.
My executors, too, should be men of good fame;
I appoint Edmund Ruffell, of Cockfield, by name;
In his old easy chair, with whort pipe and snuff,
What matter his whims, he is honest enough;
With Samuel Seely, of Alpheton Lion,
I like his strong beer, and his word can rely on.
When Death's iron hand gives the last fatal blow,
And my shattered old frame in the dust must lie low,
Without funeral pomp let my remains be conveyed
To Brent Eleigh churchyard, near my father be laid.
This, written with my own hand, there can be no appeal,
I now therefore at once set my hand and my seal,
As being my last will: I to this fully agree,
This eighteenth day of March, eighteen hundred and
three.

This amusingly self-deprecating will was made by an
antiquarian dealer, Joshua West, of Chancery Lane,
London in December 1804:

Perhaps I died not worth a groat;
But should I die worth something more,

Then I give that, and my best coat,
And all my manuscripts in store,
To those who shall the goodness have
To cause my poor remains to rest
Within a decent shell and grave.
This is the will of Joshua West.

Among all the professional people who have made poetic
wills, a place has to be found for James Bigsby, a humble
farm labourer of Manningtree in Essex, who composed
these accomplished lines in February 1839:

As I feel very queer my will I now make;
Write it down, Joseph Finch, and make no mistake.
I wish to leave all things fair and right, do you see,
And my relatives satisfy. Now, listen to me.
The first in my will is Lydia my wife,
Who to me proved a comfort the years of my life;
The second my poor aged mother I say,
With whom I have quarrelled on many a day,
For which I've been sorry, and also am still;
I wish to give her a place in my will.
The third that I mention is my dear little child;
When I think of her, Joseph, I feel almost wild.
Uncle Sam Bigsby, I must think of him too,
Peradventure he will say that I scarcely can do.

And poor Uncle Gregory, I must leave him a part,
If it is nothing else but the back of the cart.
And for you, my executor, I will do what I can,
For acting towards me like an honest young man.

Now, to my wife I bequeath greater part of my store;
First thing is the bedstead before the front door;
The next is the chair standing by the fireside,
The fender and irons she cleaned with much pride.
I also bequeath to Lydia my wife
A box in the cupboard, a sword, a gun, and knife,
And the harmless old pistol without any lock,
Which no man can fire off, for 'tis minus a cock
The cups and saucers I leave her also,
And a book called 'The History of Poor Little Mo',
With the kettle, the boiler, and old frying-pan,
A shovel, a mud-scoop, a pail, and a pan.
And remember, I firmly declare my protest
That my poor aged mother shall have my oak chest
And the broken whip under it. Do you hear what I say?
Write all these things down without any delay.

And my dear little child, I must think of her too.
Friend Joseph, I am dying, what shall I do?
I give her my banyan, my cap, and my hose,
My big monkey-jacket, my shirt, and my shoes;
And to Uncle Sam Bigsby, I bequeath my high boots,
The pickaxe and mattock with which I stubbed roots.

And poor Uncle Gregory, with the whole of my heart,
I give for a bedstead the back of the cart.
And to you, my executor, last in my will,
I bequeath a few trifles to pay off your bill.
I give you my shot-belt, my dog, and my nets,
And the rest of my goods sell to pay off my debts.

A London lawyer, Charles Smithers, evidently fed up
with a lifetime of writing boring wills, put his own
intentions into the following brief lines of verse filed in
1869:

As to all my worldly goods now, or to be, in store
I give to my beloved wife, and hers for evermore.
I give all freely, I no limit fix:
This is my will, and she's executrix.

Pat O'Kelly, a Tipperary schoolmaster, lived up to the
humorous reputation of his race with this testamentary
verse made in 1886:

I, having neither kith nor kin,
Bequeath all I have named herein
To Harriet my dearest wife,
To have and hold as hers for life.
While in good health, and sound in mind,
This codicil I've undersigned.

Few wills in either lawyers' prose or humorists' verse can
have made the testator's wishes clearer than these lines
written by Owen Powell of Cardiff in 1897:

When my Wife's a Widow of me bereft,
She shall inherit all I've left;
And when she's finished her career,
It shall then go to my Daughters dear.
In equal Shares to save all bother,
Not flesh to one and fish the other,
They are all kind and dear to me,
So no distinction shall there be.

Two American examples of wills in verse to conclude this
section – the first written by a farmer, Joseph Cassiday of
Jasper County, Missouri in March 1901:

I, Joseph Johnson Cassiday,
Being sound of mind and memory,
Do hereby publish my intent,
This my will and testament,
That all my just debts first be paid,
Expense for burial and funeral made,
And all expenses made of late,
Out of my personal and real estate.
I do bequeath, devise and give,
As long as she, my wife, shall live,
Lot six in the original town of Lever,
To her assigns and heirs forever.
To my adopted daughter Marie,
I do devise and give in fee,
The southeast quarter of section seven
Township nine and range eleven.
To my two sons Josephus and Reach,
I do devise one dollar each.
The residue of my estate,
I do bequeath to Mary Kate,
And I hereby appoint her for,
My last will, executor.
This eighteenth day of May was done,
In the year of our Lord, Nineteen One.

The most recent will in verse with its salutary remarks was made by Mrs Mamie Jordeen of New Orleans who said to her husband in 1977:

> Don't go to Vegas or play with stock,
> Or drink much after six o'clock,
> Or party far into the night;
> You'll join me if you don't live right.
> And, please, when all my songs are sung –
> Don't fall for someone cute and young.

4

ANIMAL
ANNUITANTS

Over the years a great many pets have been remembered favourably – as well as financially – in the wills of their devoted owners. Investigation seems to indicate that the first person to leave such a bequest was an eccentric French lady named Madame Dupuis who left specific instructions for the care of her *cats* in her will of 1677:

'*Item.* I desire my sister, Marie Bluteau, and my niece, Madame Calonge, to look to my cats. If both should survive me, thirty sous a week must be laid out upon them, in order that they may live well.

'They are to be served daily, in a clean and proper manner, with two meals of meat-soup, the same as we eat ourselves, but it is to be given them separately in two soup-plates. The bread is not to be cut up into the soup, but must be broken into squares about the size of a nut, otherwise they will refuse to eat it; the whole is then to be mildly seasoned, put into a clean pan, covered close, and carefully simmered before it is dished up.

'If only one cat should survive, half the sum mentioned will suffice. Marie Bluteau is to take charge of my cats, and to be very careful of them. Madame Calonge is to visit them three times a week.'

Another Frenchman, a rich landowner named Jacques Posset of Toulouse, left his fortune to his *horse* in 1781:

'I declare that I appoint my russet cob my universal heir, and I desire that he may belong to my nephew George.'

'Polly, having been my faithful companion for many years, I leave in charge of Mrs Mary Dyer of Park Street, Westminster, with an annuity of £200 to be paid quarterly. It is my condition that his existence and identity must be proved at each quarter, and that he be given quarters which are high, long, large and roomy. Should my appointee die before Polly, he should be given into the care of some respectable female who should not be a servant. He should furthermore not be taken out of England on any account.'

– A clause from the will of a Mrs Elizabeth Hunter made in 1813 relating to the welfare of her much-loved *parrot!*

A trio of pets received 'pensions' from the will of David Garland of Middlesex in June 1828:

'I bequeath to my monkey, my dear and amusing Jacko, the sum of ten pounds sterling per annum, to be employed for his sole and exclusive use and benefit; to my faithful dog, Shock, and my well-beloved cat, Tib, a pension of five pounds sterling; and I desire that, in case of the death of either of the three, the lapsed pension shall pass to the other two, between whom it is to be equally divided.

'On the death of all the three the sum appropriated to this purpose shall become the property of my daughter Gertrude, to whom I give this preference among my children because of the large family she has, and the difficulty she finds in bringing them up.'

The English astronomer, Sir James South, clearly placed a higher value on the cost of the upkeep of a *dog* as compared to that of one of his servants when he wrote his will in 1868:

'*Item.* I instruct that the sum of £30 per year be paid to M. . . . , a female servant, so that she may care for my favourite toy terrier, Tiger, who is to be produced should any question arise as to his existence. I further instruct that the sum of £1,000 per year be put aside for his care and maintenance.'

Mrs Elizabeth Balls of Streatham, England, laid down strict provisions for the care of her late husband's two favourite animals in her will of November 1875:

'I direct that my late husband's mare and greyhound should not be sold, but carefully maintained to which end I leave £65 per annum for the care of the horse, and £5 per annum for the care of the greyhound. The dog must be walked only at his own request, and the horse should be exercised not more than one hour each day, not above four days a week, and ridden only by a person of light weight.'

A wealthy French tradesman with a curious sense of humour named Thomas Heviant of Crône-sur-Marne left provision in his will of 1878 for an annual pig race in the village:

'*Item.* A bequest for a race with pigs, the animals to be ridden either by men or boys. The sum of 2,000 francs to be awarded for the winner, on condition that for two years after the competition he wear deep mourning in my memory.'

Jonathan Jackson of Columbus, Ohio, left his fortune in 1881 for the erection of a *cats' home* for which he gave precise instructions:

'It is to contain dormitories, a refectory, areas for conversation, grounds for exercise, and gently sloping roofs for climbing. There should also be ratholes for sport and an auditorium within which the inmates may assemble daily to listen to an accordian, this instrument being the nearest approach to their natural voices. To adjoin the establishment there should be an infirmary, staffed by a surgeon and three or four professional nurses.'

Another cat-lover, Miss Charlotte Raine of Woodstock, Oxfordshire, also left careful provision for her pets in her will of June 1894:

'And as regards my pussies, Titiens, Tabby Rolla, Tabby Jennefee and Ursula, they are to be left to Ann Elizabeth Matthews, who is to receive £12 per year for the upkeep of each cat so long as it shall live.

'The pussies Louise and Dr Clausman are to go to my maid, Elizabeth Willoughby, while my black and white Oscar I leave to Miss Lavinia Sophia Beck. Both are to receive £12 per year for their upkeep.

'All the remainder of my pussies are bequeathed to Ann Elizabeth Matthews, and I hereby instruct my executor to pay £150 a year out of the dividends of my father's shares in Lambeth Waterworks towards their support,

although this is not to extend to any kittens afterwards born.'

Miss Mathilda Lyons of Chichester made the following provision in her will dated September 1932 for the care of her three *goldfish*:

'And I bequeath the sum of seventy pounds per annum for the maintenance of my three goldfish. They can be identified as follows: one is bigger than the other two, and these latter are to be easily recognised as one is fat and the other lean. I also make provision for flowers to be placed upon their graves when they pass on.'

A Chicago attorney, named Patrick Wilton, bequeathed his entire fortune to his two accomplished pet dogs in 1947, instructing his executors:

'I decree that my estate of $30,000 shall be used to maintain and care for my dogs, Pat and Gunner, in the manner to which they are accustomed. They are well deserving creatures, for they can speak to me. They also enjoy watching Mickey Mouse and have well-defined tastes in literature.'

Another wealthy animal beneficiary was a pet cat belonging to Mrs Alma Culbert of St Petersburg, Florida, who declared in her will of 1958:

'And I therefore instruct that my cat, Pearl, shall be my sole beneficiary and the recipient of my holdings estimated at $23,000.'

A San Francisco millionairess who was widely believed to prefer animals to human beings confirmed this notion when her will was published in 1959. Mrs Amy Bachman wrote:

'I leave the sum of $600,000 to establish a memorial fund for my deceased terrier "Bingo".
'To the San Francisco Society for the Prevention of Cruelty to Animals, who shall administer the memorial, and the other animal charities hereunder listed, I bequeath $336,000.
'To my husband, Roger, I leave $1, and my son, nothing.'

The largest single bequest to animals was made by Eleanor Ritchey, heiress to the Quaker State Refining Corporation,

when she died in Fort Lauderdale, Florida, in 1968:

'I bequeath my entire estate, value estimated at $4.5 million, to my 150 stray dogs.'

(Perhaps, understandably, this will was contested by the woman's relatives, and by the time it was settled in September 1973, the estate had grown in value to $14 million, while the number of strays still living had shrunk to 73!)

An American dog-lover tried to protect the well-being of his pet with a special inducement in his will. Writing in 1973, Will Jonson of Maryland said:

'I hereby bequeath every damned thing I own that she wants to my wife, with the following stipulation: that my dog Lobo who is essentially the same temperament as I, be allowed more freedom than I have been allowed.'

Budgerigars have been the favourites of many old people, and one such pet was remembered in the will of Mrs Janet Fetherstone of Wolverhampton in 1980:

'I leave £200 to my friend N . . . . who has promised to love and take care of my dear little budgerigar, Pepi. She is a little dear. I love her very much. I know she will miss me.'

Perhaps, though, the most unlikely of all animals to receive an annuity was a *tortoise* named Kipper who had belonged to Miss Mary Pack of Upton, Bermuda. In her will of June 1982 she declared:

'I hereby bequeath the sum of £1,000 annually for the care of Kipper, who has been my companion for 50 years. The sum is to be paid to the local zoo on the condition that the owners provide him with a quiet home for the rest of his days.'

(*According to a later report, 'Kipper' was placed in a compound housing twelve female tortoises and the wealthy old fellow has since been making love sixty times a day!*)

5
WHERE THERE'S
A WILL

There's a Relative

The twentieth century has produced not only the
longest of all wills, but also the shortest – as well as
some of the most humorous and bizarre bequests. Each and
every one goes to prove that nothing has really changed
over the years: many modern men (and women) still find a
last laugh irresistible and where there's a will there's always
a relative!

The world's longest will was compiled by the eccentric
American newspaper tycoon, William Randolph Hearst,
who died in 1951. Although no precise details are
available, it is said to run to millions of typewritten words,
covering hundreds of thousands of sheets of paper, and be
so voluminous that it occupies several rooms!

The longest, most precisely documented will, though, was
filed in January 1925 on the death of Mrs Frederica Evelyn
Stilwell Cook, in London. Her epic list of instructions and
bequests ran to 1,066 probate folios containing 95,940
words! This extraordinary testament which must have
taken months, if not years in the making, is now bound in
four large, gilt-edged volumes!

The shortest will in the world contained just two words
and was written by an exiled Czech, Johan Tausch, of
Langen in Germany in January 1967. His quite
considerable estate was duly administered on the strength
of these words which he signed:

'Vse zene'
(Everything to my wife)

A will just one word longer had been shakily written on
an envelope by a dying man, Frederick Charles ('Charley')
Thorn of Streatham, London, on 16 May, 1905. His three
words were later accepted for probate, and his estate of
£8,000 was conveyed to his wife, the 'mother' of his will:

'All for mother.'

From the longest and the shortest wills, to the inevitable
relatives who have a habit of turning up when an
inheritance seems possible. Right at the start of the
century, in 1801 in fact, an American physician, Dr
Frederick Wagner of Connecticut, who had apparently
been totally ignored by his family for much of the time
while he was alive, gave vent to his macabre sense of
humour in his final testament:

'To my relatives who, now that I am dying, cannot do too much for my comfort, I declare as follows. That to my brother, Napoleon Bonaparte, I bequeath my left arm and hand; to another brother, George Washington, my right arm and hand; and to my brother Lord Nelson my legs, nose and ears. And to this end I leave one thousand dollars for the dismembering of my body.'

This amusing clause appeared in the will of another doctor, Ian MacIntyre of Glasgow, published in 1902:

'To my wife, as a recompense for deserting me and leaving me in peace, I ask that my sister, Elizabeth, make her a gift of ten shillings sterling from my bequest, so that she is enabled to buy a pocket handkerchief to weep after my decease.'

An evidently hard-done-by American wife, Mrs Mary Burns, of Rochester, New York, got her own back on her husband with these words in her will made in 1903:

'Mr Burns has not ever paid his marriage expenses to his wife. Mr Burns on his way to church had to borrow $5. In days of sickness as well as of health, the husband

did not bring the least joy to his wife. Wherefore he is a curiosity. He never treated her to anything. She honours him now with $5 as he deserves it.'

Katherine Moody, a beautiful and much admired young southern lady from Kentucky, who died tragically young in 1904, requested in her final testament:

'Over my grave I desire that tobacco should be planted, so that weed, nourished by my dust, might be smoked by my bereaved lovers.'

A crochety old soldier, General Hawley, who also had something of a sense of humour, drew up his own will in London in 1907 because, he said, 'of the hatred and suspicion with which I regard all lawyers'. The document was accepted for probate, and in it the General left:

'The sum of £100 to my servant Elizabeth Buskett because she has proved herself a useful and agreeable handmaid.

'The remainder of my property I bequeath to my adopted son, Arthur, provided that he is not foolish enough to marry the said Elizabeth – in which case neither is to inherit a farthing.

'I further desire my executors to consign my carcase to any place they please, and if the parish priest should claim a burial fee, they may let the puppy have it.'

A superstitious rural farmer in Finland, Mat Jurgen Weins, who had apparently led an evil and dissipated life, took what he obviously considered to be the only course of action when he came to dispose of his property in his will, dated 1909:

'Having no family or relatives that I know of, and being desirous of making the best possible impression on him whose company I expect to share in the next world, I hearby bequeath my property, such as it is, to his Satanic Majesty, the Devil.

'Should any claimant on my estate present himself after I am gone, and my executor have any doubts as to my intentions, I rest assured that my inheritor will know well enough how to dissuade such a claimant.'

(Strangely, though an heir to Weins' farm was found, the man was so terrified by the threat contained in the will that he refused to lodge any claim against its provisions!)

Mary Piper, a wealthy widow of Kansas City, Missouri, ingeniously revenged herself on her nephew, Rollins Bingham, who had at first been a favourite and then displeased her. In her will of 1910, she declared:

'I do leave to my nephew Rollins Bingham, the sum of $2,500 to be held in trust by my executor *until the death of my nephew and then applied to give him a proper burial.'*

A wealthy attorney, Robert G. Dryenforth, of Washington DC, was obsessively anxious to prevent his young foster son, Robert St George Dryenforth, falling prey to the 'wiles of women', and laid down the following conditions in his will of July 1910 which the boy (then 8 years old) had to follow to the letter if he was to succeed to his father's large estate when he reached 28:

'I particularly request my executors to thoughtfully and well guard my beloved son from women, and sensibly, that is, gradually, through no erratic extreme, to let him be informed and know the artful and parasitical nature of most of the unfortunate sex, and to care that he does not marry beneath him.

'He must not associate with one Jennie Dryenforth, or her daughter, Rose Marie Knowlton. Should he do so, the estate goes to William H., Harold, and Robert Dryenforth, who are named as executors.

'The above named three executors will also share the estate in the event Robert St George thoughtlessly dies before he reaches the given age.'

An habitual drinker, E. J. Halley, of Memphis, Tennessee, divided what was left of a fortune he had inherited from an eccentric aunt among various acquaintances including a number of baseball players (his favourite sport), several bar tenders (who had supplied him with drinks), and three deputy sheriffs (who had seen him safely home when he was drunk). He also remembered several drinking companions, and, with notable generosity, two other people who helped him at what must have been critical moments – as his will of October 1910 vividly reveals:

'To the nurse who kindly removed a pink monkey from the foot of my bed – $5,000.
'To the cook at the hospital who removed snakes from my broth – $5,000.'

A will allegedly written by a ghost was filed for probate in the Supreme Court of the District of Columbia,

Washington DC on 12 August, 1910. Mrs Elida J. G.
Crowell presented to the court what she claimed to be a
translation of an illegible message written by the spirit of
her husband, William H. Crowell, a clerk in the Treasury
Department, after his death. The 'will' read:

'Dear Elida,
'This is what I tried to write on a slip of paper, I want
my brother, W. H. H. Crowell, Washington, U.S.A., to
be my executor if I should pass away with my sickness. I
have perfect trust in him. I believe he will deal honestly
with my children. I have set aside $5,000 for the
exclusive use of my wife. Give little Elizabeth and her
brother William both $100 to put in the Savings Bank.
'Ruby met me. I have seen many folk here. This is a
beautiful world. Is better than the Sixth Auditor's office.
They can't put me out here. (Signed) W. H. Crowell.'

(Perhaps needless to say, the will was rejected.)

A French restaurant owner, Pierre Giffard, developed an
abiding dislike for his fellow-countrymen, and made this
very evident in his will filed in Marseilles in 1911:

'I declare that the French are a nation of dastards and
fools, and I therefore bequeath the whole of my fortune

to the people of London. I also desire that my body should be taken from this country and deposited into the sea a mile from the English coast.'

George Crowfield, a rich Manchester bachelor who had been persistently urged much against his will to get married by members of his family and relatives, made this specific request in his last testament dated 1913:

'I beg that my executors will see that I am buried where there is no woman interred, either to the right or to the left of me. Should this not be practicable in the ordinary course of things, I direct that they purchase three graves, and bury me in the middle one of the three, leaving the two others unoccupied.'

Martin Willow, a Londoner, found an ingenious way round a strange legacy bequeathed to him by an uncle in 1917. The will declared:

'To my nephew I leave the sum of £2,000, but on condition that half of this sum is to be placed beside me in my coffin and buried with me.'

Having assured himself from the executor that he would receive the money as long as the condition was carried out, the astute young man wrote out of a cheque for £1,000 and gave it to the lawyer to place alongside his uncle's body. On it he wrote, 'Pay to Bearer'.

A London merchant banker, William Hampton, of Kew, anxious to impress upon his young son the need for careful study of financial matters, wrote in his will of 1918:

'I leave to my son a copy of *Lawrie's Interest Tables*, not for its intrinsic value, but in the hope that so small an incident may be of use to him in future years. And I particularly recommend to him the study of the compound interest tables, as showing that from comparatively small investments, by patience, large sums may be realised.'

Benjamin Werner, a millionaire Austrian, who had a life-long fear of darkness, made the following extraordinary provision in his will published in Vienna in 1921:

'Insomuch as I have a profound horror of darkness, I desire that my executors see that the vault in which I am

placed is continually lighted by electricity, and that my coffin is similarly illumined, to which end I leave all the proceeds of my estate herebefore listed.'

An eccentric Bordeaux lawyer named Claude Benoit whom many people had expected to leave his large fortune for the building of a school or municipal building in his memory, lived up to his reputation for doing the unexpected when his will was filed in 1926:

'I hereby direct and command that my executors convey the whole of my property, estimated at 100,000 francs, to the construction of a lunatic asylum, for I believe this to be an act of restitution to the clients who were insane enough to employ my services.'

A father, obviously unhappy at his daughter's choice of a husband, made what he must have felt was a fitting bequest in his will of 1927. James Harrow of Kensington declared:

'To my daughter I leave the sum of one hundred sovereigns which she is to spend on herself.

'To my son-in-law I leave my old walking stick in the hope that someone will give him a good thrashing.'

Daniel Ross of Michigan was remembered as the archetypal hen-pecked husband. He managed to have the last word, however, when he made his will in 1928:

'For my tyrannical wife, who did not give me any peace during the last twenty-four years since I was married to her, I leave ONE DOLLAR for which to buy a rope and hang herself. There was not a married man yet more miserable.'

Arguably the most generous will of all was that of Wilson E. Stoudt, a resident of Los Angeles, made in 1930 – though his claim to ownership of the estate in question was debatable to say the least:

'To Mrs Charlotte L. Stoudt, I give and bequeath all that certain Parcel of land from the Atlantic to the Pacific with all the trees and every living thing thereon.
'And to Charles L. Stoudt, Jr, I give the Four Winds of the Earth, that he may Enjoy them the same as I have.'

By contrast, a Scottish widow named Maud Galloway left the smallest sum possible by way of legacies to a number of her late husband's relatives who had clearly made her life extremely trying while she was alive. In her will, published in 1934, she declared:

'To those relatives herebefore mentioned, I therefore bequeath the sum of One Farthing each as a reward for their mean scheming for years.

'And to K. . . . L. . . . , that dangerous, intriguing female, that Arch Schemer, also the sum of one farthing, that she might remember when she wanted to compel me to buy her old hats at £1 each.'

One of the queerest bequests of this century must surely be that made in July 1935 by an American lady, Ellen Collins, of Philadelphia, who instructed that a piece of her underwear be given to a male friend:

'I give, devise, and bequeath my white flannel embroidered petticoat, made by Mrs Lowry, to Mr Albert Cummins absolutely.'

(Unfortunately there is no record as to why Mr Cummins might have longed for this item, for he died before coming into his unusual inheritance!)

A man who planned to 'enjoy' his death was Lazar Kutovich, a wealthy property owner in Belgrade, Yugoslavia, who declared in 1937:

'In death I wish to have the comforts which for so many years were denied to me in life. Therefore I am setting aside 100,000 dinars to be buried sitting up in an armchair with a table, cigarettes, matches and my first wife's photograph beside me.'

The will of 98-year-old Lewis Evan Morgan of Gwyllgyth, in Glamorgan, written in 1941, was generous and to the point, though hardly flattering:

'I give to my faithful old servant, Ester Jones, the whole that I am possessed of either in personal property, land, or otherwise. She is a tolerable good woman, but would be much better if she had not so clamorous a tongue.'

The owner of a women's dress shop in Brighton, England, Andrew Evans, avenged himself on a nephew who had persistently teased him about his occupation, with this clause in his will published in 1948:

'And to C. . . . H. . . . , I bequeath the sum of £200,

but before receiving it he must, in the presence of my executor, walk down the most important street in our fashionable resort dressed in female attire.'

'I do herewith bequeath to nurse Lillian Pelkey and nurse Madeline Higgins from my estate the sums of $10,000 to be paid on my death. Given with my hand on 9 August, 1948.'

Unexceptional though those lines may seem, they were actually written by a generous old American, George W. Hazeltine, on a pair of knickers belonging to one of the nurses, Lillian Pelkey! As he lay dying at the age of 86, the old man told the two nurses who had looked after him in a Los Angeles hospital that he wanted to leave them something for their kindness to him. Although they protested, he insisted, and as there was no writing paper to hand, nurse Pelkey hoped to humour him out of his plan by offering her knickers. Not at all taken aback the jolly old soul took up the offer and created one of the sauciest wills of the century. Although Lillian Pelkey wrote the bequest and Hazeltine signed it, it was ultimately rejected under California law by a judge who clearly did not appreciate the old man's sense of fun!

Wane Gordon, a doctor of Portland, Oregon, made a number of generous bequests to relatives and friends in his will of 1959. But when it came to his fellow doctors and nurses he added:

'To all of them I bequeath a lusty belch.'

Continuing the honourable tradition of having the last word on those nearest and supposedly dearest, American banker Evan Abrahamson said in his will of 1964:

'To my wife I leave her lover and the knowledge that I wasn't the fool she thought I was.
'To my son I leave the pleasure of earning a living. For twenty-five years he thought the pleasure was mine, but he was mistaken.
'To my valet I leave the clothes he has been stealing from me regularly for ten years.
'And to my chauffer I leave my cars. He has almost ruined them, and I want him to have the satisfaction of finishing the job.'

Patriotism was demonstrated in the most positive terms by Miss Marjorie Jesson of Bournemouth, Dorset who, after a

number of bequests to her family, completed her will in 1971 with the words:

'And the remaining sum of £20,000 I bequeath to the Chancellor to assist in the repayment of the national debt.'

By far the most gruesome last testament made in recent years must be that of a London baker who died in 1972. Harold West gives every sign of having believed in vampires, for he asked his executors to carry out 'most precisely' these instructions:

'My doctor is to drive a steel stake through my heart to make sure that I am properly dead. And when I am buried my coffin is to be nailed shut in case I might still be breathing and thereby make an escape.'

Philip Grundy, a Lancashire dentist, demonstrated the same unbending attitudes as his famous forebear, Mrs Grundy, when his will was published in March 1974. For to inherit the major part of his fortune of over £180,000 his unmarried nurse had to observe the following conditions:

'That she must never use any lipstick or any other make-up of any kind whatsoever apart from clear nail varnish, and wear no jewellery such as rings, earrings, necklaces, and never go out with any men on her own, or with a party of men, during a period of five years. I want her to be happy, as she has been a real friend to me – and genuinely had my interest at heart.'

Edward Horley, a bachelor of Altrincham, who had spent a long and hard life working as a coal merchant, bitterly resented the money he had had to pay the tax man. He expressed this anger in his will of 1975, instructing his solicitor:

'Take what is left from my estate after the duty is paid and buy a lemon. This is to be cut in two: one half sent to the Income Tax Inspectorate and the other to my Tax Collector. With each, add the message, Now squeeze this!'

Two motorists obviously very strongly attached to their favourite cars gave instructions in their wills recently to have the vehicles buried with them! In August 1975 when Mrs Margaret Griffiths of Ladybrand in South Africa died, she left these directions:

'To bury with me my 1948 Studebaker Champion so that it might also rest.'

(There was, however, strong opposition to this request on two counts. The car was said by collectors to be a rare item – one of only nine left in the country. While the undertaker protested he could not bury the blue vehicle because 'the cemetery is for whites only'.)

The second devoted driver was the young widow of a Texas oil millionaire, Mrs Sandra West, of San Antonio, who in March 1977 left her entire $2.8 million estate to her brother-in-law, Sol West, as long as he complied with the following conditions:

'To dress my body in a lace nightgown and place it in my favourite car, a blue 1964 Ferrari, with the seat slanted comfortably.
'Should the said Sol West fail to carry out this request, he is to inherit only $10,000.'

(Although, again, this will was disputed by relatives, a Los Angles court ruled that the instructions should be carried out and Mrs West was duly buried in the Ferrari which was placed in a steel container and encased in concrete.)

A retired teacher, Ernest Digweed, of Portsmouth, made one of the most celebrated wills of recent years in 1976. After a lifetime spent living quietly in a small terrace house, and with no known relatives, he left his estate of £25,107 in trust:

'To be paid to the Lord Jesus Christ in the event of a Second Coming. My estate is to be invested for 80 years, and if during those 80 years the Lord Jesus Christ shall come to reign on Earth, then the Public Trustee, upon obtaining proof which shall satisfy them of his identity, shall pay to the Lord Jesus Christ all the property which they hold on his behalf.'

(A further clause in the will stated that the accumulated interest on the estate was to go to the Crown after twenty-one years, and if Christ had not appeared within eighty years the Crown was to inherit everything.)

Jack Greenslade of Berkshire, whose life-long passion was horse racing, could not bear the thought of missing his beloved sport even in death, and requested his executors in his will made in 1981:

'I did not miss an Ascot Race Meeting for 40 years, and ask that my ashes be scattered on the winning line so that I can watch the winners go by.'

A keen amateur footballer, Sid Trickett, of Torrington in Devon, asked for his final resting place to be on the ground where he enjoyed his greatest moment of triumph. In his will of March 1982 he instructed his family:

'To scatter my ashes in the goalmouth at Torrington football ground where I headed eight goals in 1948.'

An American sea fisherman, Don Mobelin, of New York, thought he might continue to be of use to his fellow anglers after his death, and gave special instructions to his executor in his will of 1983:

'I request that my ashes be thrown onto the shoals of New York bay where I have often fished with my friends of the Bronx Fishing Club in the hope that they might attract the fish and enable me to give my friends one more good catch.'

A similar outrageous sense of humour was revealed in the will of Tony Gribble of Bristol who asked in his will of June 1983:

'That my ashes may be used in the family's egg timer so that I shall continue to be of use after my death.'

And, finally, my own favourite humorous will - which I might well have written myself if Tom Goodison of Norwich in Norfolk had not thought of it first in April 1983 – who asked for all his relatives and friends attending his funeral to be given an envelope containing a one pound note on which were written the instructions:

'Have a smoke and crack a joke. Thanks for coming. '

241

DIED LAUGHING

or
One Last Goodbye!

For

JOHN KENT

– may the spirit be with us always!

PREFACE

You've probably heard the joke about the man who died laughing – well, it actually came true in March 1975. A jovial Scotsman named Alexander Mitchell got such a chuckle from his favourite television comedy programme, *The Goodies*, that it killed him.

His wife Nessie explained afterwards that one of the sketches which involved a fight between a black pudding and some bagpipes had set Alex off.

'It tickled my husband and he just kept laughing non-stop throughout the whole half-hour programme,' she said. 'It was nearly over when he collapsed.'

Mrs Mitchell told the press that she bore the comedians concerned no hard feelings – in fact she was even going to write to them thanking them for making her husband's last minutes so happy! And she added, 'I have often said, "I nearly died laughing", but I never thought it could happen. It is incredible.'

Incredible it certainly is. But though death is invariably sad, it sometimes comes, as in this case, with a touch of humour. And that in a nutshell (or a coffin, if you prefer) is what this collection of last moments is all about. For herein you will find a lot of dead funny tales that I have collected from all over the world and spanning the past eighty odd years. (I've stuck to the twentieth century to avoid a volume the size of the *Domesday Book*.) They range from the actual moment of passing to some pretty ghastly interventions from the spirit world. Each story has also given the person concerned a little slice of immortality – for it should be stressed that every one of them is true!

Sometimes the humour is almost unintentional – like the case in November 1976 of an off-duty Missouri fireman, Gary Miller, who died in a fire which broke out in his home while he was asleep. In the ruins of his house was found a smoke detector which had obviously been awaiting installation. It was ringing dutifully.

Sometimes it is of a much blacker kind, as in the instance of a 30-year-old Florida TV newsreader, Miss Chris Chubbock, who suddenly announced on her programme in July 1974, 'In keeping with Channel 40's policy of bringing you the latest in blood and guts and in living colour, you are now going to see another first – attempted suicide.' With this, Miss Chubbock pulled a gun from under her desk and shot herself in the head. She died fourteen hours later without regaining consciousness.

And on still other occasions it reaches the level of pure farce. I quote the story of the ham-fisted French safe-cracker who was shot and killed by gendarmes after a night of trying to break into a Paris bank safe in 1978. Only afterwards was it discovered that the safe had been accidentally left unlocked all the time!

Just occasionally, too, the jaws of death don't quite snap shut – and you end up with hilarious instances like the group of Chinese refugees who tried to commit suicide in 1982 after being refused permission to settle in the Philippines. Rather than return home, the men poured over themselves what they thought to be petrol and then tried to set it on fire. Only after several matches had been unavailingly applied to the

'petrol' was it discovered that it was, in fact, fish sauce!

Of course, there have also been some very amusing last words from people on their death-beds, and I believe that a section of the best of these warrants a place in this book. And add to them some of the quite hilarious words of valediction pronounced on the not-always-so-dear-departed by those involved in their passing and you have a laugh-a-page assembly about that one moment we *all* have to face one day.

From these remarks I am sure you will gather that my book is a pot-pourri of dying moments that also happen to be very much a laughing matter. Together I think they prove that even where there is death there can still be a touch of humour. (If not, you'll know this is one De'ath to avoid on the cover of future books!)

So, if you will, please enjoy One Last Goodbye. . .

Richard De'Ath
October 1984

1
WORSE TO COME

'There's worse to come' has proved literally and often grimly true, and there are few better examples with which to begin a section of the more outlandish cases of this kind than the story of Major Walter Summerford.

In 1918, while fighting in Flanders, Major Summerford was struck by lightning, thrown from his horse, and as a result of his injuries was invalided out of the Army.

Six years later, back in his native Canada, he was hit again by lightning while fishing near Vancouver. And in 1930 all the odds about lightning never striking twice, let alone three times, were overturned when another bolt struck him and left him paralysed!

Major Summerford died in 1932 and was laid to rest in a secluded grave not far from Vancouver. Then, two years later, nature played her final trick – a shaft of lightning struck the poor Major's grave and completely shattered his headstone!

During an outbreak of fighting at an isolated outpost on the Mons front also during the First World War, a German soldier named Heinz Müller shot and killed an English soldier in the opposing trenches.

Later, as Müller advanced with some other German troops to the English lines, he found the body of the man he had killed still upright, his rifle aimed to fire and his now cold finger still poised on the trigger.

Deciding to take the dead man's rifle as a souvenir of his

success, Müller wrestled with the stiff fingers to release the weapon. As he did so, the rifle suddenly went off and shot him dead through the heart!

When Abe Bonham, a sharecropper of Cotter in Arkansas, returned from a shopping trip in August 1928 he saw smoke billowing from his small wooden home.

Quickly, Abe recruited help from other sharecroppers living nearby and with their assistance was able to salvage a good many items from the burning building, as well as finally bringing the flames under control.

Just before the fire was put out, however, there was a sudden report. A gun which Abe always kept loaded in the drawer of a bureau had been set off by the flames.

And, tragically, it was Abe who was in the way of the stray bullet – he fell dead at the feet of his friends.

As David Anthony was driving home to Liverpool in March 1936, he suddenly came around a sharp bend and found to his horror another car racing towards him on the wrong side of the road.

Desperately, David slammed on his brakes, but his car skidded uncontrollably and the two vehicles collided head on.

When David regained consciousness in hospital, he was thankful to learn he had escaped the terrible accident with only minor cuts and bruises. The other motorist had also miraculously survived.

But there had been a passenger in the other car and he was dead. And the unfortunate man turned out to be David Anthony's twin brother, Paul . . .

Some weeks after Igor Ravenko had undergone a stomach operation in Moscow in 1949, he returned to hospital complaining of more abdominal pains. For a second time he was operated on, and the medical team discovered the previous surgeon had inadvertently left a pair of clamps in Igor's stomach.

Happy at this discovery, Igor returned to his family. A month later the poor fellow was dead.

At the autopsy he was opened up once more. And this time in his stomach was discovered a surgical gauze pad which the second surgeon had left behind!

Luigi Ercolli chose the most horrendous way of committing suicide in 1959 – he decided to set fire to himself on a deserted headland not far from his home in Nardo, southern Italy.

No sooner had he begun his grisly ritual, however, than Luigi had second thoughts. Frantically, he began to roll about on the ground and beat at the flames.

In his terror, though, he forgot where he was – and suddenly fell over the edge of the headland and plunged to his death on the rocks below . . .

The most bizarre case of a near-fatal motoring accident occurred in the Ténéré desert in the Niger, in 1960.

A French soldier, Henri Le Queux, was driving an army lorry across this vast, sandy wilderness when he rammed a tree and overturned the vehicle. Reports said he was lucky to escape with his life.

The tree was the only one within a radius of fifteen miles!

A persistent lover in Hamburg, West Germany, refused to heed warnings about the crazy lengths to which he was going to impress his loved one.

He would clamber over roofs to see her. Shin over high walls merely to catch a glimpse. And even hang from wires outside the office where she worked.

In July 1963, the exasperated police finally gave chase when they spotted the boy on the roof of the girl's home. As he ran, the youth suddenly slipped and fell 75 feet down a chimney.

A few minutes later he was found with his neck broken – lying in the fireplace of his girl's bedroom.

While suffering from acute depression, Walter Alexander, a Chicago engineer, drove to a local motel in March 1966 intent on committing suicide. In one of the bedrooms he took out a revolver and shot himself three times in the head.

Some hours later Walter awoke to find he was still alive and feeling rather better. He decided to return home and tell his wife the injuries to his head had been caused by a fall. Miraculously, all three bullets had passed straight through his head.

A week later, however, Walter received a visit from the police. They had found the three bullets from his revolver in the wall of the motel bedroom.

On admitting to his incredible escape from death, he was promptly charged with causing criminal damage.

David Lee, a Canadian scientist, met a tragic end in 1967, when he was decapitated because he did not bend low enough as he was climbing into a helicopter and had his head cut off by the rotor blades.

Later, the case came to court – and the Quebec magistrates ruled that Lee's estate must pay for the damage done to the helicopter!

Californian Carol Hargis set out with dedicated and ingenious efficiency to kill her unfortunate husband, Harry, in 1968.

First, she gave him a massive dose of LSD. This did no more than give him a mind-bending trip.

Next, she dosed a blackberry pie with the venom of a tarantula – but still he survived.

Equally unsuccessful was sabotaging his car with a home-made bomb (it failed to go off) and attaching a live electric wire to his shower.

Once again she returned to poor Harry's food – dosing his beer with tranquillisers, but he thought the drink was off and threw it away. When he fell ill from all these unpleasant attentions, Carol even tried injecting air into his veins.

She finally succeeded in her objective and earned a life sentence – by the simple expedient of striking him on the head with an iron bar.

Tired of all the violence in the streets of her native Belfast, Mrs Elizabeth McClelland emigrated around the world to New Zealand in 1970.

Tragically, just two years later, in February 1972, Mrs McClelland was rushed into a Christchurch hospital suffering from head injuries from which she subsequently died.

Police inquiries established that her injuries had been

caused by being struck on the head by a placard carried by a demonstrator who was protesting on behalf of Irish Civil Rights.

The death penalty is applied for several crimes in Saudi Arabia – persistent theft being one of them.

A young burglar in the town of Jiddah was prepared to take the risk when he thought he had found a foolproof way to beat the security bars on the windows of a luxury block of flats. So, in March 1972, in order to get through these bars, he took off all his clothes and his shoes.

Inside the apartment block, however, the naked youth was suddenly surprised by a returning resident and had to flee. His initial delight at having avoided an appointment with the executioner by his cleverness suddenly turned to horror, though, when a thought flashed into his mind.

In the pocket of the trousers he had left behind . . . his identity card!

After his wife had left him, John Stratton of Manchester saw no point in going on living. He decided to commit suicide in 1973, and having carefully sealed the doors and windows of his home, turned on the gas oven.

Although the fumes soon engulfed the house, because the

supply was North Sea gas, they proved non-toxic. This lucky escape made Stratton have second thoughts. Perhaps he would give life another chance. He took a cigar from the mantelpiece and lit it.

At this, the highly inflammable North Sea gas exploded him and his house into smithereens.

David Falconer had been growing ever more depressed during the months of 1974. And it seemed to make no difference what his friend Sharon Payne did or suggested – he grew still more gloomy.

Then, one night as the couple sat in Falconer's Los Angeles apartment, he pulled a pistol from under a cushion, thrust it against his temple, and pulled the trigger.

The horrified Sharon could only watch in terror as the bullet killed her friend, passed through his head, ricocheted off a wall, and then struck her right between the eyes. She never recovered consciousness.

As Woodrow Creekmore was driving to his home in Chickasha, Oklahoma, in 1976, his car suddenly slewed across the road and hit a telegraph pole. Amazingly, he was able to get out of the virtually demolished vehicle without a scratch.

However, as he stood discussing the accident with a police patrolman who appeared on the scene, the telegraph pole suddenly toppled over and, striking Woodrow on the head, killed him instantly.

In February 1976, a Belgian doctor, Herman le Compte, claimed that he had devised a rejuvenation treatment which would enable people to live for 1,000 years.

The police were not impressed by his statement that he was able to arrest the natural deterioration of the body's organs by massive injections and exercise – and arrested him. He was placed in jail in Bruges to await trial for practising medicine while debarred.

Then while he waited, 'Dr Long Life' – as he was nicknamed – suffered a heart attack . . .

When Billy Vecchio of Chicago stole a car to impress his girlfriend in August 1976, he ended up with a very different ride from the one he had expected.

During his little outing, the car broke down and Vecchio hailed a passer-by to give him a push. The man, Joe White, just happened to be the real owner of the car!

Vecchio, however, laughed at the other man's claim and proceeded to punch White, a night-club bouncer by profession, on the nose.

Before he repossessed his vehicle – White later explained to a local court – he broke both Vecchio's wrists, fractured his jaw, and then stabbed him. The joy-rider subsequently died of his injuries.

According to the Detroit Free Press, in July 1977, Mr Michael Maryn of Passaic in New Jersey had been mugged eighty-three times during the previous five years.

He had been shot twice, stabbed, coshed, lost part of one ear, had his nose broken, his ribs smashed and his skull fractured. In addition to his injuries, he had lost numerous bags of groceries, four cars and over $2,000 in cash.

'I don't worry about it,' Mr Maryn told the newspaper, 'I'm lucky in one respect – I have a blood clot in my leg that keeps me from travelling far from home.'

An Italian named Abel Ruiz felt the world had ended when he was jilted in June 1978.

In his despair he hurled himself in front of the Genoa-Madrid Express. But, miraculously, he fell between the rails and sustained only minor injuries.

After being treated at the Genoa hospital, the self-destructive Abel tried suicide a second time. This time he leapt in front of a lorry. Again, he was only slightly injured by the impact.

Following further treatment at the hospital, he was only
released on the understanding that he would not try to kill
himself again.

But, within the hour, he was back once more. This time,
though, the incident was a genuine accident: he had been
struck by a runaway horse. And now his injuries *were*
serious.

The following day the man who wanted to commit
suicide was dead – accidentally!

After weeks of excruciating pain from toothache, a
market trader from Leeds named Walter Hallas could stand
it no more. But his fear of dentists was such that he could
not bring himself to seek expert help.

Instead, in December 1979, Walter went to one of his
workmates and asked him to punch him in the jaw in the
hope that would dislodge the offending molar.

The punch did just that. But Walter was also knocked
over by the blow, struck his head on the ground as he fell,
and died of a fractured skull!

Like many people, Herman Holt worried about his
income tax. Indeed, when the 55-year-old chip shop owner
from Halifax, Australia, received a letter from the Revenue
in 1980, he became convinced he had fallen foul of the

authorities and decided to kill himself rather than face disgrace. The following day he was found dead by a railway line.

In actual fact the letter had nothing to do with arrears – it was the Revenue admitting they owed *him* A\$1,400!

For several years, Herbert Foster, a chemist in Auckland, New Zealand, campaigned to have a pedestrian crossing immediately in front of his shop re-sited. He argued that the position was a 'potential death trap' and that someone would surely be killed.

They were. On 19 October 1980, just a week after Herbert had delivered yet another tirade about it in the local paper, he himself used it to cross the road and was struck and killed by a passing car!

After months of trying to find a job, Romolo Ribolla grew so dejected he decided to kill himself. On the morning of 4 April 1981, as he sat in the kitchen of his home near Pisa, he suddenly produced a gun from his pocket and told his wife he was going to shoot himself.

For nearly an hour, the distraught woman pleaded with Romolo until, overcome with emotion at her entreaties, he burst into tears and flung the revolver to the floor.

But as it struck the ground, the gun went off and shot Mrs
Ribolla dead.

A man described as 'The Most Accident-Prone Person in
Britain' made a habit of spending every Friday the
thirteenth in bed for his own safety, according to a report
published in November 1981.

For in the space of five years, Robert Renphrey, a
Peterborough bus driver, had suffered one calamity after
another on this fateful Friday. He had been:

Involved in five car crashes and four bus breakdowns.

Fallen into a river and been knocked down by a
motorcycle.

And even walked through a plate-glass door!

Giuseppe Saraniti was convinced his wife was having an
affair with Salvatore Manganaro. And in March 1983 he
confronted the other man in his home in Genoa, Italy,
brandishing a revolver.

Falling to his knees, Salvatore swore that the story was
not true. He had never touched Maria Saraniti. But
Giuseppe was not convinced and thrust the revolver
against the frightened man's temple.

Salvatore closed his eyes and clutched at the gold
pendant of the Virgin Mary hanging around his neck.

'Mother of Jesus,' he pleaded, 'give him a sign I am telling the truth.'

Giuseppe pulled the trigger. But nothing happened, only a dull click.

Now it was Giuseppe's turn to be frightened and he ran to the police station in Genoa and confessed what he had tried to do. After he had been charged with attempted murder, a police spokesman said, 'The strange thing was there was nothing wrong with the gun. It was fully loaded and worked perfectly when we tested it!'

Vittoria Luise loved his little three-wheeled bubble car and firmly believed it was his good luck charm – a much safer vehicle to ride in than ordinary cars. And on 6 February 1983, as he was driving alongside the river Sele near Naples, he had reason to believe his faith was well founded.

For a sudden gust of wind caught the little car and bowled it over into the river. Before it struck the water, however, the door flew open and Vittoria was flung clear, to be able to swim safely back to the bank.

Once on dry land, he was just congratulating himself on his narrow escape – though bemoaning the loss of his precious car – when another gust of wind blew a nearby tree down on top of him, killing him instantly.

A man aptly named Hi Woe was rushed naked into a
hospital in Peking in February 1983 with a metal spittoon
stuck on his head.

According to the ambulancemen who brought him in, the
spittoon – a common item in Chinese bedrooms – had
been playfully plonked on his head by his wife while the
couple were making love.

Although the doctors battled hard to save the young
man's life, he died of asphyxiation before he could be freed.
Later, it was learned the previous evening had been his
wedding night!

Mike Stewart, the president of the Auto Convoy
Company in Dallas, Texas, was so convinced of the
dangers that a number of low-level bridges in the city
presented to traffic, that in April 1983 he decided to make
a movie about the problem to convince the authorities.

Hiring a camera crew, he proceeded to drive around
Dallas on the back of one of his trucks to film the potential
death spots. As he did so, the truck went underneath one
of the bridges in question and he was decapitated.

An attractive 16-year-old Israeli girl was taken to court in Tel Aviv in September 1983 and ordered to stop walking around her home in the nude.

The complainant was not a neighbour, but the girl's 80-year-old stepfather. Her provocative displays were to give him a heart attack, he said, so that she could inherit his fortune!

George Schwartz was a conscientious worker and with Christmas coming up, he decided on the evening of 10 December 1983 to put in some extra hours at his factory in Providence, Rhode Island.

Suddenly, as he worked, a huge explosion ripped the factory apart, and by a miracle George was thrown clear by the force of the blast. As he crawled away, he saw through the falling masonry and flames that only one wall of the factory was still upright.

After being treated for his injuries and shock, dedicated George returned to the remains of the factory to see if he could salvage any of the papers and files he had been working on.

As he was rooting through the debris, that sole surviving wall collapsed and crushed him to death.

Football fan Felix Gill was not enjoying watching his team Athletico Madrid play on 7 March 1984. For a start, the 70-year-old had had a row with his wife about going to the game.

Now Madrid were taking a beating at the hands (and feet) of their old rivals from Barcelona.

Then poor Felix slumped into a coma with a brain haemorrhage.

And there he stayed in his seat for *a day and a half* before he was discovered and rushed to hospital!

A shopping trip for a little old West German housewife in the city of Wuppertal in July 1984 turned into a catastrophe.

Having made her purchases, Frau Martha Harbou returned to her car. She smiled to herself at the sight of her pet cat still asleep on the back seat where she had left her.

But no sooner had she begun to drive off, however, than the cat suddenly leapt up and bit her. Frau Harbou screamed and lost control of the car.

At once the car careered into a parked lorry and then demolished a sausage stand. This, in turn, dragged a fish-frying stand over, burning an assistant with boiling fat. Pedestrians everywhere scattered as Frau Harbou's car finally smashed into a wall.

The unfortunate lady died shortly afterwards in hospital. The cat escaped without a scratch.

A French couple appeared in court at Bobigny near Paris in September 1984 charged with trying to murder each other.

The 60-year-old husband had been awoken suddenly in the night by a severe electric shock. Leaning over the bed was his wife, who was wearing rubber gloves and had attached an extension lead from the mains to his head. Over his heart a wet sheet had been laid.

Leaping from the bed, the man rushed to the next room, seized a rifle, and returned to shoot his wife in the thigh.

In court, it was explained that the man's poor eyesight had saved the life of the wife. And the electric shock had failed to kill him because the couple lived in one of the few streets in the area where Electricité de France provided a lower-powered system with less than the normal 220 volts which *would* have proved fatal!

2
FATEFUL TALES

Fate has played some cruel – and deadly – tricks on mankind. Take the case of New Yorker Joseph O'Malley. He was exceedingly drunk one night in 1953 and decided to take a short cut home along a subway railway line. When, inevitably, nature called, O'Malley decided to pee right where he stood. Unfortunately, when the stream of urine hit the third rail of the track, 600 volts shot up into his body and he dropped dead.

While working on a farm near Ahmedabad in western India, in 1957, a labourer accidentally fell into a deep storage pit full of cow manure.

Six other labourers who also jumped into the pit to try to rescue the man suffered the same fate – suffocation.

Because thieves were constantly stealing apples from her orchard, Mrs Laura Baines of Penzance in Cornwall decided to employ a nightwatchman to keep an eye out for the pilferers.

Unfortunately, Mrs Baines did not trust her employee and one night in 1959 she crept out into the orchard to make sure he was not asleep on the job.

The man shot her dead.

An elderly Swedish pastor met an unlikely end while engaged on church duties in the winter of 1955.

Pastor Karlo Toivio was baptising some new members of his church at the time – standing in a pool of heated water for the ceremony. Things went fatally wrong when his assistant clergyman handed him a live microphone . . .

Devoted birdwatcher Henry Humphret of New York was finding extreme difficulty in 1963 in getting near enough to some swans living on High Shield Lake to ring them. In desperation, he decided to try to approach them by night in disguise.

Obtaining the hollowed-out body of a swan, he placed it over his head and waded into the lake just after midnight. Unfortunately he could not swim and drowned in the darkness.

An eccentric Californian inventor, Reuben Tice, of Monterey, was obsessed with creating a machine for taking the wrinkles out of prunes.

In November 1967, having perfected a piece of equipment which he hoped would perform such a task, he set it in motion. A mighty explosion followed.

Tice was discovered dead under the shattered remains of

his machine and a huge pile of prunes. They were all still wrinkled.

Horror struck the Brazilian town of Goiânia in December 1973 when a column of killer ants a mile long and half a mile wide marched into the community. It took sixty firemen with flame throwers over fifteen hours to drive the ants back into the jungle.

In their wake they left the scant remains of several people they had devoured – including the chief of police.

So distraught did Mrs Vera Czermak of Prague become over her husband's infidelities that she decided to commit suicide from the window of her third-floor flat. On the morning of 25 July 1975 she hurled herself out . . . and landed on Mr Czermak who was returning unexpectedly to the flat. She survived unhurt – he was killed.

Another man killed by an unlikely falling object was Araldo Anastasi, a pensioner, who was returning home to his fourth-floor apartment on Rome's Via dello Scalo, in February 1954.

Waiting excitedly for his return was his little terrier dog,
Leo, who yelped with pleasure at a window when the old
man came into sight in the street below.

Unfortunately the little creature overbalanced, fell from
the ledge, and landed on top of his master – killing him
outright.

Wishing to enhance her tan, American sunbather Mrs
Linda Saverd lay out on a sheet of aluminium foil stretched
over a chaise-longue at her New Jersey home, in August
1975. The idea was that the foil would intensify the sun's
rays.

It did – and Mrs Saverd cooked herself to death in a
temperature of nearly 110 degrees Fahrenheit.

A freak storm ended six years of drought in the Spanish
Sahara in August 1975, leaving behind it a number of giant
pools of water.

Into one of these, Mohammed Aliud fell and died –
drowned in the middle of the desert.

Felix Hanaud, a 77-year-old Frenchman who had always

received excellent medical care during his lifetime, decided to donate his body to science by giving it to the Toulouse University Medical Faculty.

In February 1976, some years after he had drawn up his will, Felix went into the University building, told the caretaker he could wait no longer – and shot himself through the head.

There was nothing that General Miguel Arracha, the head of the Anti-Urban Guerrilla Section of the Argentine Army, enjoyed more than a game of dominoes. Indeed, it was his habit to play each week at his home in Buenos Aires with a friend, General Carlos Mendoza.

But this came to an abrupt end in June 1976 when General Arracha was blown to pieces by a bomb that his friend General Mendoza left behind after one of their games!

Cricket has long been one of the great passions of the people of Pakistan, but in 1976 this passion got completely out of bounds during a match between two rival teams in the north of the country.

One of the umpires, Karim Singh, gave a number of decisions which were highly controversial and caused the tempers of the fielding side to rise to the point of rage.

When, once again, Singh refused a clear-cut appeal for leg

before wicket, several of the fielders grabbed the stumps from either end of the pitch and furiously beat the umpire to death!

Thoughts of love and romance were on the mind of honeymooner Philip Ryan as he walked back to his holiday cottage on Reunion Island in the Indian Ocean, in June 1977. He had taken a short stroll in the moonlight while his bride of one day was preparing for bed.

With a gleeful love call Philip vaulted over what he believed to be the fence surrounding the cottage – and disappeared into the crater of the Ganga volcano.

Keen angler José Hermanez accidentally struck a bees' nest with his line while fishing from the banks of the Rio Negro not far from São Paolo, in August 1977. The infuriated bees immediately attacked José.

To escape, he leapt into the river – and was promptly devoured by piranha fish.

After undergoing a successful operation to have a replacement heart in November 1977, Mr George Least, a dairyman of Salisbury, Rhodesia, fell in love with a nurse

who helped him through his convalescence.

When the girl did not return his love, Mr Least shot himself.

Former actress Eleanor Barry, 70, could not resist hoarding every newspaper, press cutting, book and souvenir which in anyway related to her career. Over the years, this collecting mania grew to such an extent that the house she shared with her sister in New York became jammed from floor to ceiling.

On 20 December 1977, she was found dead in the house – a huge pile of the books and newspapers had fallen on her.

Charged with aiding a suicide, salesman Marvin Redland told a curious story to a court in Norfolk, California, in December 1977. He had been discussing reincarnation with the barmaid of a club in town.

The woman had first told him she had been a canary in her previous life. The next time she returned to earth, she told Redland, she would be a buffalo.

'I admit that I laughed in her face,' the witness said. 'Greatly to my surprise she then shouted, "You may laugh, but I will prove it." At this she reached under the bar, took out a gun, and shot herself dead.'

A Canadian cabaret entertainer called 'Le Grand Melvin', who dressed as a vampire and performed an act with boa constrictors, missed a trick during his act at La Tuque in Quebec, on 22 August 1978.

One of the 7ft 6in long snakes wrapped itself around the entertainer's neck, and when the club manager saw him turning blue in the face called the police.

'I had to cut off the snake's head,' the manager said later. 'It wasn't a pleasant thing to do. Unfortunately, "Le Grand Melvin" was already dead.'

An Australian snooker fan who desperately wanted to have a shot named after him spent years trying to come up with a new variation. In January 1979, Robert Fairtree of Melbourne finally cracked the problem.

He announced the 'Fairtree' which was made by a man suspended over the table with his legs fastened to the ceiling and helium balloons attached to his wrists. Sadly, when Robert gave a demonstration he crashed on to the table and died.

As a dutiful Chief Justice of New Guinea, Sir William Brown was not averse to visiting the scene of a rather unusual traffic accident which had occurred in Papua in

April 1979. He was accompanied by members of the jury and also the accused motorist, Mr Morrie Modela.

While the group stood discussing the events, however, they were suddenly startled by the appearance of a number of local tribesmen who emerged from the trees. They were even more surprised when they attacked Mr Modela and hacked him to death.

A Sri Lankan woman's attraction for a snake proved fatal in Trincomalee in 1980. She had raised a cobra in the belief that it was her dead son reincarnated.

On 1 July the snake bit her and she died.

Two out-of-work Italians were both desperate to land the job as a waiter which had just come vacant in a Naples restaurant in August 1981. As both Fathir Ziouni, 23, and Lofi Aunadni, 22, were scared the other would land the position, they agreed to fight a knife duel on the lonely beach at Latina, south of Naples – winner to take all.

But neither claimed the vacancy. Fathir died, stabbed through the heart, and Lofi was imprisoned for murder.

Attempts to find the oldest man in Asia in 1982 finally
brought to light a 118-year-old Malaysian with the
extraordinary name Lebai Omar Bin Datuk Panglima
Garang. Nor was that all that was extraordinary about him:
he was also living in sin with a teenage girl.

To celebrate his record, the old man agreed to marry the
girl. However, on his return from the wedding ceremony
riding a tandem which some well-wishers had given him,
with his wife on the front, Lebai Omar fell off and died.

There was an unexpected finale to the screening of some
pornographic films in Manila in February 1983, which were
being shown to raise money to finance an international
film festival in the Philippines.

One man died of a stroke – and another was shot dead by
his wife, jealous at the sex scenes he had watched.

A fetish for washing women's hair was the undoing of a
29-year-old Italian, Luigi Longhi, when he was brought
before a court in Soenderborg, Denmark, in March 1983.

Luigi was said to have had a life-long craving for female
tresses, and was confined indefinitely for strangling Heike
Freiheit, a 21-year-old West German hitch-hiker, whom he

had tied up and then washed her hair four times before killing her.

Sixteen-stone assistant manager James Ferrozzo was enjoying an off-duty hour with one of his dancers, Teresa Hill, in the topless Condor Club, San Francisco, on the night of 22 November 1983. All the customers had left after a hectic evening, and Ferrozzo lay down on the top of a trick baby grand piano beside the girl.

Inadvertently, a switch was triggered which caused the piano – normally used in an erotic cabaret – to be raised up and down to the ceiling. Unaware of what was happening until it was too late, Ferrozzo was squashed to death – only his bulk saving the young dancer beside him.

'She was so intoxicated she doesn't even remember getting on the piano,' a police officer said afterwards.

During a football final between two Calcutta teams held in November 1983, over 30,000 spectators went on the rampage. Police were called in to stem the pitch invasion and stop the bloody fights which broke out all over the ground. In the riot, one man was shot dead.

The cause of all the trouble had been an offside decision given by one of the linesmen.

The most unlikely murder weapon was exhibited in a trial held in Wellington, New Zealand, in April 1984.

Before the court was 53-year-old Malcolm Francis, charged with beating his wife to death with – a frozen sausage. He denied the murder.

Olympic marathon hopeful, Richard Mbelwa, 22, of Dar es Salaam in Tanzania, had put in many hours of arduous training. As he was running through a golf course on the morning of 10 May 1984, a policeman suddenly ran into sight and shot him dead.

The officer said later he thought Mbelwa was a fleeing thief.

Turkish authorities decided to ban the screening of video tapes in buses after a tragedy in Ankara, in June 1984.

An offended bus driver had tried to turn off a love scene on a video while he was driving along. In the ensuing accident seventeen people were killed.

Two Chicago lawyers arguing the respective merits of certain athletes in forthcoming Olympic Games in July

1984 decided to settle their dispute by racing each other down a hallway in their law firm.

One of the men, who had poor eyesight, crashed through a 39th-floor window and fell to his death.

An Italian with an eye for beautiful girls could not resist the temptation offered by a private nudist beach near his home in Naples. One day in July 1984, 48-year-old Salvatore Ancoretti climbed up to a rock high above the beach and with his binoculars ogled the nude sunbathers below.

In his excitement, though, he forgot to check the rock for safety – and when it gave way he plunged 100 feet to the beach. He died on impact – still clutching his binoculars.

A 34-year-old Yugoslav, Vebi Limani, died near his home on Sara Mountain in August 1984 when he was struck by lightning.

Reporting his death, the local newspaper *Politika* said he was the fourth member of his family to die in the past six years. His father, brother and uncle had all passed on – similarly struck dead by lightning.

Three parachutists attempted a spectacular trick jump before thousands of spectators in Denver, Colorado, in August 1984. They were planning to float to the ground one above the other.

Instead, the top man dropped on the parachute of the man below and both fell on the third jumper. All three were killed.

Barbecuing was one of the passions shared by Diane Fellman and her husband, Jim, at their palatial American home in San José.

But when they fell out of love in August 1984, Diane shot poor Jim. Afterwards she cooked his body on the barbecue and ate part of his arm.

There was a curious sequel to a murder case in Los Angeles in September 1984. A mother of 61 who had buried her murdered son the previous year instituted proceedings against the police claiming damages of $500,000.

She claimed that the law still had her boy's skull.

Torrential rain had left hundreds of Indians homeless in the Assam area, and they waited with increasing anxiety for relief supplies in September 1984.

When a helicopter finally reached the flood victims to make a drop, two people were killed and three others injured when they were hit by the falling food packets.

Fifty-seven-year-old Edward Hill was feeling pretty chipper as he left a Houston hospital in November 1984. He had just spent three weeks being treated for a minor heart complaint and was now declared fit.

As he crossed the foyer he was handed his bill for the treatment. He took one look – and dropped dead. The bill was for $38,000!

3
IN MEMORIAM

Over the years there have been some very apt and often humorous comments passed 'In Memoriam'. Here are some of the best of them.

The most bizarre final comment was surely that of a convicted English murderer, Edgar Edwards, as he was led to the scaffold in December 1902, condemned to death for killing John and Beatrice Darby.

As he mounted the steps, he said brightly to the hangman, 'I've been looking forward to this!'

Two American Army buddies were chopping wood together on fatigue duty at Fort Smith, Arkansas, in June 1922. Suddenly, Private Daniel McGranie remembered that his friend, Private Benjamin Clark, owed him ten dollars. He demanded the money back there and then.

Both men stopped chopping and an argument ensued. Clark denied ever having borrowed the money and refused McGranie's insistent demands.

All at once McGranie lifted his axe and with one blow severed his friend's head from his body.

'I just lost my head,' was all he could mutter as he was taken in charge.

A deranged New Yorker, Ernest Walker, not only

committed a totally motiveless crime in 1949, but also left
an equally bizarre confession at the scene of the crime.

Walker lured a young messenger boy to his Manhattan
apartment and clubbed him to death with an iron poker.
He then left the body for the police to find with a note
scrawled upon it:

'I expect you will be surprised to see what I have done.'

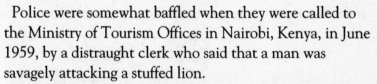

Police were somewhat baffled when they were called to
the Ministry of Tourism Offices in Nairobi, Kenya, in June
1959, by a distraught clerk who said that a man was
savagely attacking a stuffed lion.

The officers arrived to find the man pummelling the lion
and shrieking abuse. He had apparently smashed the glass
cage in which it was on display and then tried to strangle it.

Said one of the policemen later, 'When the man calmed
down he told us his brother had been killed by a lion and
he wanted revenge!'

Mischievous little 3-year-old George Semple was being
taken for a walk along the cliffs at Brighton, in Sussex, by a
family friend in 1960, when he tumbled over and was killed
on the rocks below.

Later, the friend confessed to the police that she was responsible, having pushed George over. 'He just would not behave,' she said.

Few learner drivers showed more determination than Mr David George of Shanklin, in the Isle of Wight. Then immediately upon being told he had passed his test in July 1976, he collapsed over the wheel of his car and died.

'It was his eighth attempt,' a sad instructor said later.

Another man who had success snatched from his grasp at the moment of triumph was an American, Johann Crispet of Washington, who died in August 1976 on the day before he was due to be awarded a licence to practise law. What was also remarkable about Mr Crispet was that he was 102 years old.

'He always wanted to practise at the bar,' said his son later. 'Before he died he had taken the requisite examinations twenty-six times!'

In order to emphasise the terrible nature of hanging, D.H. Beenan, a leading opponent of capital punishment, was

demonstrating just what happened when it took place to
an audience in New Zealand, in 1976.

Slipping a noose which he had hanging from a rafter
around his neck, Mr Beenan exclaimed, 'How horrible the
whole thing is!' – stepped from the chair he was standing
upon and accidentally hanged himself.

As he was taking photographs of the city dump of
Takapuna, also in New Zealand, for a new brochure in July
1976, photographer Peter Hammond became conscious of
a bulldozer coming in his direction. Anxious not to
interrupt the driver's work, Mr Hammond stepped behind a
pile of rubbish.

At this – said a policeman later giving evidence into Mr
Hammond's death – the bulldozer driver brought his
vehicle closer and with incredible delicacy squashed the
photographer into the ground.

The driver later told the law, 'I hate snoopers.'

In February 1977, a West German housewife, Hilda
Brunner of Frankfurt, was charged with murdering her
husband by putting rat poison in his daily glass of beer for a
period of four years.

She confessed to the police, 'I only did it to cure him of drinking.'

It was an open and shut case when Michael Koukourakis appeared before a court in Piraeus, Greece, in September 1977, charged with murdering his wife's lover.

Michael was very ready to admit he shot the man to death, but pleaded, 'I acted in an instant of momentary sanity.'

The jury agreed and acquitted him.

When a group of Brazilian policemen raided a party in Santiago after complaints that it had been going on noisily for three days in May 1978, they found rather more than they expected. For sitting upright in one corner was a dead man.

Asked to explain, the host of the party said, 'He was a gate-crasher called José. We discovered that he was dead on Saturday evening. But not wanting to spoil the party we decided to leave him there until Monday morning.'

French farmer Pierre Trichard of Mexmieux was happily

watching a game of World Cup football on television in
June 1978 when his wife, Claudi, asked him to shell some
peas for their supper.

Pierre refused, and despite several further entreaties,
continued to stare resolutely at the TV set. At this, Claudi
snatched her husband's shotgun from the wall, took aim,
and blew his head off.

'I couldn't understand it,' Mme Trichard said later,
'France were already out of the competition.'

Football also shattered the happy home life of a
Yugoslavian couple in August 1982. While Marinko
Janevski, a retired policeman, was watching a match on
TV at his home in Belgrade, his wife came into the room
and tried to stop him.

'I strangled her,' Marinko later admitted while standing
trial for murder. 'I always get excited when watching
football.'

While Mrs Barbara Eastman was selling flowers in
Naysmith Square, Toronto, in September 1978, she was
suddenly approached by a man who announced: 'I am God
– could you direct me to the nearest church, please?'

Although somewhat taken aback, Mrs Eastman gave the

necessary instructions and then watched in amazement at what happened next – for as she later explained in court:

'When I had given him the directions he took off his hat, said "Thank you", stepped out into the road, and was instantly killed by a tractor.'

All his life, keen angler Jerry Head of Melbourne, Australia, had dreamed of catching a giant-size fish. When he did, it literally killed him – as his wife Rhoda told newpapermen in November 1978, after the family had marked his passing in a rather unusual way.

'He was out fishing with my son Doug when he landed a 58-pound cod,' said Mrs Head. 'The shock killed him. But after the funeral we had a fish supper – cod-fritters on a bed of clams with his name written in instant potato over the lot.'

After the unfortunate death of her father, Mrs Joan Spence gave evidence at a London inquest in March 1980.

'My father died after slipping on a bacon sandwich,' she told the court. 'As he was a life-long vegetarian I consider this to be a manifestation of divine injustice.'

The familiar situation of a husband falling out with his mother-in-law took on a new dimension in India, in April 1980.

For when Vekay Velayudhan appeared in a court in Poona charged with beheading his mother-in-law, he said simply in his defence: 'We had not been getting along for some time.'

Problems can also arise between parents and children – but hardly as bizarre as that which occurred in America, in October 1980. Before a New York juvenile court appeared 14-year-old Christine Martin who said that because her parents had complained when her pet rabbit left droppings on their living-room carpet, she picked up her father's gun and shot them both to death.

'I have been having problems with them for some time,' she calmly added.

Mr Harry Olsen was understandably upset at the death of his wife, the former Miss Stella Walsh, an Olympic Gold and Bronze Medallist, who passed away at their home in southern California in December 1980.

But he was stunned by the revelation of the post-mortem that his 'wife' was, in fact, a man!

'We had been married for almost thirty years,' he said afterwards. 'I am 92, but I must have been a lot more innocent then than now.'

The 'shooting' of arch-villain J.R. Ewing in the television soap opera *Dallas* provoked as many heated arguments as to who was responsible both on-screen as well as off. In Dallas itself, in March 1981, a couple named Silverstone took their argument to the limit in a grim reprise of the show itself.

So angry did the wife become at her husband's refusal to agree with her verdict on who was JR's killer, that she walked out of the living-room, fetched a shotgun, and slayed her husband.

'She was under some strain,' a relative told police later.

A South African judge with the singularly appropriate name of Justice W.J. Human was addressing a man who had been found guilty of rape, in August 1983.

Sentencing the prisoner, Rodney Axe, to death, he added, 'I have treated you as leniently as possible.'

At an inquest in Sheffield, Yorkshire, in October 1983, into the death of a Mr Harry Tanner, evidence was given by his brother who had watched the whole incident.

John Tanner said that his brother had climbed to the top of a 200-foot-high bridge and then with a wave of his hand and a shout of 'Geronimo!' had plunged to his death in the river Tees.

'He was a happy-go-lucky chap,' added Mr Tanner.

A quickstep became a 'danse macabre' in a fashionable Dallas nightspot called Ianni's Club, in May 1984, when a man became enraged. For no apparent reason, the dancer shot his partner and then went on a spree, killing five more people.

A police spokesman said later, 'He pulled a pistol and shot several people. He left, went to his car, reloaded, came back and shot some more!'

Faces were red in Fort Lauderdale, Florida, when a letter was sent out by the local social security office in June 1984 to a woman of 61 who had died the previous December.

The letter, to a Mrs Pat Shamres, six months after her death, contained a handwritten addition which said, 'We have received a report that you may be deceased. Please come in with proof of identity.'

4
EXIT LINES

And now a few last words from the famous, beginning perhaps inevitably with Oscar Wilde (1854-1900) who, true to his reputation, is credited with not one but two exit lines on his death-bed. So you may take your choice from either.

'This wallpaper is killing me. One of us must go.'

Or else:

'Alas, I am dying beyond my means.'

The great South African statesman, Cecil Rhodes (1853-1902), took his final confinement with ill-concealed annoyance and his final words were to one of his secretaries:

'Turn me over, Jack.'

The enormously influential Russian playwright, Anton Chekhov (1860-1904), who died at the height of his powers had a suitably dry comment to make:

'It's a long time since I drank champagne.'

(Appropriately, the great man's coffin then rode to burial in a freight car marked FRESH OYSTERS!)

The brilliant American short story writer, O. Henry (real name William Sydney Porter, 1862-1910), went out of this vale of tears quoting from a popular song:
'Turn up the lights. I don't want to go home in the dark.'

Efforts to make the great Russian writer and mystic, Leo Tolstoy (1828-1910), seek comfort from the Russian Orthodox Church as he lay on his death-bed were met with this sharp rejoinder – which was also his last:
'Even in the valley of the shadow of death, two and two do not make six.'

The energetic 26th President of the United States Theodore Roosevelt (1858-1919), slipped gracefully away with these words to those grouped around his bed:
'Put out the light.'

Robert Erskine Childers (1870-1922), author of the classic spy thriller, *Riddle of the Sands* (1903) and a member of Sinn Fein, said, as he was about to be executed, with other patriots, by an Irish Free State firing squad:
'Take a step or two forward, lads – it will be easier that way.'

The famous English novelist, Arnold Bennett (1867-1931), died in Paris of typhoid after drinking a glass of water. His last words were:

'The water is perfectly safe.'

Thomas Edison (1847-1931), the American inventor and man of vision, chose to look forward rather than back in his last words, informing those around his death-bed with tantalising emphasis:

'It's very beautiful over there.'

Oliver Wendell Holmes (1841-1935), the great American judge, delighted in telling the story of the last moments of one of his uncles, John Holmes, who died in Boston. As the man lay on his death-bed, a nurse who was busy keeping his feet warm was heard to remark, 'If his feet are warm, he is alive – nobody ever died with his feet warm.'

At this, John Holmes suddenly sat up in bed and said, 'John Rogers did!' Then he died.

(John Rogers was an English Protestant burned at the stake for heresy in 1555.)

One of the finest British men of the law of this century,
Lord Chief Justice Gordon Hewart (1870-1944), passed
away on a fine spring morning with these words ringing
around his room:
'Damn it! There's that cuckoo again!'

The irascible film comedian and lifelong agnostic W.C.
Fields (1880-1946) was found reading the Bible on his
death-bed. Asked the reason for this astonishing
about-face, Fields grumbled:
'I'm looking for a loop-hole!'

One of the funniest men of the twentieth century,
humorist James Thurber (1894-1961), who shrugged off
the blindness that inflicted his last years with comments
like, 'I don't get distracted by the sight of a pretty girl but
of course I can still hear a pretty girl go by,' did not
disappoint his admirers with his last words:
'God bless . . . God damn!'

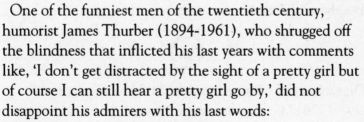

The rumbustious Irish writer and notorious drinker,
Brendan Behan (1923-64), passed his last remark to a nun
comforting him on his death-bed:

'Ah, bless you Sister, may all your sons be Bishops.'

When the pioneer woman Member of Parliament and socialite, Nancy Astor (1879-1964), found herself surrounded by her children as she lay dying in her bed she demanded of them:
'Am I dying or is this my birthday?'

Tallulah Bankhead (1903-68), the American actress and a celebrated wit, was economical in her use of words and amusing in her demand when she died in New York City's St Luke's Hospital.
'Bourbon,' she said.

That master of wit and humour, Sir Noel Coward (1899-1976), did not disappoint his friends and admirers when it came to making his final *bon mot*:
'Goodnight, my darlings, I'll see you tomorrow,' he said.

'The King of Rock 'n' Roll', Elvis Presley (1935-77),

despite the torment of his closing years, remained a devout Christian to the end, and his last remark was singularly appropriate:

'We'll make this tour the best ever.'

American Pulitzer prize-winning author William Saroyan (1908-81) actually went to the trouble of telephoning the Associated Press with what were to be his last words:

'Everybody has got to die, but I have always believed an exception would be made in my case. Now what?'

The distinguished British comic actor, John Le Mesurier (1912-83), employed his gentle, irreverent sense of humour when he left instructions for the following announcement of his death to be published in the Personal Column of *The Times* newspaper:

'JOHN LE MESURIER wishes it to be known that he conked out on November 15th. He sadly misses family and friends.'

The famous English comedian and magician, Tommy Cooper (1922-84), who collapsed and died while appearing

on stage during a live television show, passed on joking just
as he had done in life.

At the end of his act he held up a black square of rubber
and said, 'This is an Irishman's bowling ball.'

And as the audience chuckled, he ad-libbed, 'I thought it
would get a bigger laugh than that.' It was the last joke he
ever made.

As Oscar Wilde opened this section with two exit lines, it
is perhaps only appropriate to close in the same manner –
though it is equally open to debate whether the humorist
in question used either remark attributed to him.

Much-loved comedian Eric Morecambe (1926-84) said in
February 1981 that he would like to be remembered as a
skilful fisherman and hoped his last words would reflect
this.

'I don't talk much about it now,' he said, 'because I blush
easily. But I hope people in the future will appreciate my
genius – particularly with pilchards – and how I beat the
handicap of having an apprentice with short and hairy
gumboots.'

In November 1983, after he had twice overcome heart
attacks he was again asked how he would like his obituary
to read. Eric replied with characteristic speed:

'See. I told you!'

5
GHASTLY SPIRIT

The goings-on of those who have passed over can also have their funny side, as the spirited stories in this section will show.

Take, for example, the amorous ghost who began paying his attentions to a pretty, 18-year-old Manchester girl, Sarah James, in March 1965. According to Sarah, her invisible lover would announce himself to her as she lay in bed with a gentle kiss on the shoulder. Then she would feel the touch of his hands on her body under the bedclothes, and finally the sensation of someone getting into bed.

'I just let him do what he wants,' Sarah declared. 'And he does it beautifully . . . he can certainly love!'

But when Sarah's mother, Jane, grew alarmed at these stories and decided to change places with her daughter and sleep in her bed . . . nothing happened.

The randy wraith preferred blondes, it was decided.

The doctors at a New York hospital were amazed when a 41-year-old patient, Donald Cohen, suddenly leapt out of his bed in March 1968. Their amazement was understandable: Donald had had two heart attacks and the specialists had given him up for dead.

But that wasn't the only amazing thing about his recovery. He had a bizarre story to recount of his experiences 'on the other side'.

'I dreamt I was on a merry-go-round,' he said, 'and the

angel of death was beckoning me. The carousel picked up speed, but I managed to resist the mysterious force that pulled me towards him.

'I jumped off – and found myself on the floor of the hospital ward!'

A Swedish doctor has devised the strangest set of scales imaginable, according to a report published in 1969. Dr Nils Olof Jacobson believed it was possible to weigh the human soul and set about proving his theory by placing the hospital beds of dying patients on extremely sensitive scales.

From his research, said Dr Jacobson, he had established that at the precise moment of death the scales registered a decrease of just eight-tenths of an ounce!

Ugandan witch doctor, Dada M'Shuma, became famous throughout his country in the 1970s as 'The Man Who Can See The Future'. The old man was said to be able to make contact with the dead and also predict events that were to come.

Millions were said to believe implicity in Dada, according to a report – but sceptics claimed he got his knowledge of world affairs from a transistor radio hidden in his hut . . .

Anton Kjowski, a Polish immigrant who lived in Manchester, was obsessed with an ancient superstition that he had brought with him from the 'old country' he left over a quarter of a century earlier. He believed in vampires.

And because the traditional method of guarding against attack from vampires was to keep plenty of garlic about the house, Anton doubled his defences by sleeping with a clove of garlic in his mouth. Tragically, he was racked by coughing one night in April 1973, dislodged the piece of garlic, and was choked to death by the clove.

According to a 'Vampire Census' carried out by the Vampire Research Centre in New York in April 1983, there are thirty-five people in the United States who consider themselves to belong to the ranks of the Living Undead.

Of these people, a third lived in the state of California and one is an alien vampire – having emigrated from Spain.

A ghost with a fascination for sexy movies made his presence felt in a cinema in Bury, Lancashire, in 1976. Nicknamed, 'Old Sid', the spectre had a habit of appearing whenever X-rated films were shown.

'Old Sid' had been seen around the cinema for many years
– but less in recent times until the advent of more explicit
movies. Several times he was spotted dressed in medieval
clothes and a three-cornered hat, hovering about six feet
over the stalls.

Apparently what 'Old Sid' *didn't* like were horror movies . . .

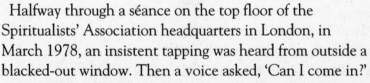

Halfway through a séance on the top floor of the
Spiritualists' Association headquarters in London, in
March 1978, an insistent tapping was heard from outside a
blacked-out window. Then a voice asked, 'Can I come in?'

The medium holding the séance promptly asked the
spirit's name and voice replied, 'Ken.'

For a moment there was a puzzled silence among those
taking part in the séance, and then the voice spoke again:
'I've been repairing the roof and somebody's locked the
window on me. Let me in!'

At this everyone present collapsed into laughter, said
secretary Tom Johanson later, and the 'ghost' was promptly
let in from 'the other side'.

'Fred', the ghost who was reported to be haunting the
Sapsford family of Larkfield, Kent, in August 1978, was a
rather unusual kind of spirit – a high spirit, in fact. For

according to the four people he suffered from B.O.

For fourteen years, the Sapsfords had been aware of 'Fred' who usually made his presence felt by the unmistakable odour of sweaty feet. At other times he left behind the scent of sizzling bacon, burnt toast and roast coffee.

Said Mrs Joan Sapsford, 'We don't want him exorcised – just sanitised.'

The Ghost family come in for a fair amount of joking. In fact there are several people with the name of Ghost, and one, Mrs Violet Ghost of London, said in 1979:

'We get a lot of phone calls from people taking the mickey. They ask if we could pop round and haunt a house for them. Some even ask if we really *are* spooks. Even my doctor used to sing "Holy, Holy, Holy" when he saw me coming!'

One relative changed his name by deed poll to get away from all these jokes, added Mrs Ghost. 'He was a solicitor and had to put up with a lot of laughter in court!'

But she still thinks it's a splendid name. 'When I'm introduced to people they always remember me. They never forget having spoken to a Ghost!'

A ghost found his way into a court in Albany, New York, in September 1979 – if only in spirit.

A couple, who were being sued for reneging on an agreement to purchase an old house built in 1857, claimed they changed their minds after discovering the place was haunted.

In the interim, however, new purchasers had been found: although they had so far seen nothing, it was reported. But they *were* anxious for an encounter, as the man explained. 'We hope it's the kind of ghost that moves furniture around for we could sure use the help!'

Another ghost made its presence felt in a court in Palm Beach, Florida, a few months later in January 1980.

Things began to go bump in the night after a 56-year-old millionaire shot himself in Jim and Corinne Succhi's villa, the court was told. Explained Jim, 'The doors opened and shut, water taps started to gush, electric lights flashed on and off, and at midnight we were roused by terrifying screams.'

He and his wife were suing the millionaire's heirs for $100,000, claiming they suffered fear and sleepless nights in the haunted home.

Defending the case for the heirs, attorney James Waters said, 'I've heard of paying guests, but not paying ghosts. Even if it's true that my dead client haunts the house, he has every right to spook where he pleases.'

And the judge agreed.

A Californian mystic, Sande Marsolan, founded a Ghost Adoption Society, in February 1980, offering clients the chance to become friends with famous spirits from the past such as Shakespeare and (can you believe it?) Attila the Hun!

According to Ms Marsolan, she has had the gift to communicate with ghosts since she was five, but it takes her three hours of intense concentration to reach specific spirits. Among the eighty-five spirits she had called up was a beautiful female ghost from the Renaissance era who shared the prison cell of a man in San Quentin – that is until she began playing tricks on the guards!

For her $150 fee she also made contact with the ghost of the Marquis de Sade who was wanted to 'liven things up' in a Los Angeles hair salon.

Unfortunately, Ms Marsolan had to be hastily summoned back to get rid of the randy Marquis when he apparently began a persistent bout of pinching the bottoms of the young girl assistants!

This same year also saw another 'spirited' offer made to American believers in the supernatural.

The May 1980 issue of a spiritualist magazine said that astral love-making was now available. For $1,000, a group of mediums offered clients a chance to once again make love to partners who had passed on!

When the President of Italy's Magicians' Association, Antonio Battista, lost £1,000 in cash, a camera and over 200 letters from clients, from his car in January 1982 he took immediate action against the thieves.

Antonio had large warnings posted up on hoardings all over the town of Avellino in southern Italy where the robbery had occurred. These told the culprits that unless the stolen items were returned within three days, then he would work his magic and put the 'Evil Eye' on them.

Twenty-four hours later, Battista's magic had worked – but not completely. The letters were returned safely wrapped up in a plastic bag. But the thieves kept the camera and the cash!

In June 1982, two American psychics claimed that it was the spirit of Adolf Hitler that had masterminded the Argentine invasion of the Falkland Islands.

The men claimed that the one-time Führer of the Third Reich had not lost his 'insane drive for world domination' and was doing his best to influence conflicts wherever he could find them. The psychics said they had learned all this from seeing visions of Hitler who was being kept active in his after-life by hormones!

A wave of fear spread over the Inkomazi district of the Transvaal in the autumn of 1982 when the emaciated figure of Lamkhtswa Mhlongo was suddenly seen about the area after an absence of seventeen years. It was generally believed that Mhlongo had been eaten by a crocodile so that this must surely be his ghost!

At last, one brave man approached the 'spirit'.

'Oh, no, I'm not a ghost,' the other grinned. 'I've been in Swaziland – I ran away to become a witch doctor!'

For almost a year it wasn't the thought of the treatment that they might get in a West German dentist's surgery that terrified his patients – but the possibility of being haunted by a ghost named 'Chopper'.

According to reports, 'Chopper' – who was never actually seen – would shout insults in a staccato voice at patients sitting in the surgery at Neutraubling in Bavaria. These remarks would issue from power points, light fittings or even pieces of surgical equipment. Sometimes the words the spirit used were highly suggestive in tone.

But the loquacious phantom turned out to be an elaborate hoax. And in December 1983, 62-year-old dentist Dr Kurt Bachseitz was fined DM 12,400 in a local court for staging the trick. His 17-year-old assistant, Claudia Judenmann, had been the 'voice' of 'Chopper'.

Just to close on a cheerful note – there's love and sex after death according to an American ghost hunter named Stanley Wojcik of New Jersey. He revealed in 1984 that ghosts engage in love-making just like ordinary mortals, and also go to the cinema, like to ride in cars and aeroplanes, and even enjoy parties!

'Spirits are just like human beings,' he said his research had shown. 'They are the astral counterparts of their former mortal selves. Sex after death is not biological. Spirits do make love, but it's an all-cellular love – a blending of their energies!'

THE END

(Or is it?)

315

GRAVE MOMENTS
or
Dead But Hardly Buried

For

JACO GROOT

The Flying Dutchman – with thanks

PREFACE

For a number of years I have had a copy of a sketch, made towards the end of the eighteenth century, called 'The Merry Undertakers'. It caught my fancy originally because it happens to mention a forebear of mine, Robert Death, who was the owner of a popular tavern called 'The Falcon' located in London at the corner of the Wandsworth Road, leading towards Battersea Bridge.

In those days, the inn stood among trees and it was obviously a haven much used bv travellers in and out of the capital. Contemporary accounts also say that Robert Death was a man 'whose figure ill comported with his name, seeing that it displayed the highest appearance of jollity and good condition'. No doubt the good Robert was at his best the day the artist of the picture, 'a merry-hearted fellow named John Nixon', passed by, for Nixon was evidently much amused at the sight of a company of undertakers enjoying themselves at 'Death's Door' – as the same account amusingly puts it – and promptly captured the scene for posterity.

There is also a reference to this picture in Robert Chambers' famous *Book of Days* (1863) which, when I came across it some years ago, provided the germ of the idea for the collection of grave moments gathered here. Let me quote for you Chambers' description of 'The Merry Undertakers':

> Having just discharged their duty to a rich nabob in a
> neighbouring cemetery, they had, the first time for
> three or four hours, found an opportunity of refreshing
> exhausted nature; and well did they ply the joyful
> work before them. The artist, tickled at a festivity

among such characters in such a place, sketched them on the spot, and his sketch was soon after published, accompanied with a cantata from another hand, of no great merit, in which Sable, the foreman of the company, is represented as singing as follows, to the tune of 'I've kissed and I've prattled with fifty fair maids':

Dukes, lords, have I buried, and squires of fame,
And people of every degree;
But of all the fine jobs that came in my way,
A funeral like this for me.
This is the job
That fills the fob,
O! the burying a nabob for me!
Unfeather the hearse, put the pall in the bag,
Give the horses some oats and some hay;
Drink to our next merry meeting and quakery's increase,
With three times three and hurrah!

Chambers ends his account with what seems like a touch of regret. 'Death has now submitted to his mighty namesake,' he says of my ancestor, 'and the very place where the merry undertakers regaled themselves can scarce be distinguished among the spreading streets which now occupy this part of the environs of the metropolis.'

I've often thought how I would like to have joined old Robert and drunk along with him and his buryin' friends. But if such a thing is impossible, I can at least keep his spirit alive by showing that uproar and undertakers, fun and funerals, chuckles and cemeteries still go hand in hand, and though you might imagine that most things to do with death and burial are invariably grim, you'll learn very much to the contrary in the pages which follow.

Nor are the grave moments of which I speak merely things of the past. Any business which can currently boast a man named 'Colonel Cinders' (in California, naturally!) who performs the last rites for more than 14,000 people a year – and members of the dear departed who have recently asked to be laid to rest in tombs shaped like a minaret, a piano and even a sports car, can hardly be said to be entirely without humour!

If anybody typified the idea that there could be something to laugh about in a graveyard it was Joseph Grimaldi (1779-1837), the world's most famous clown, who was renowned for his performance as the cemetery night-watchman. His memoirs, edited by Charles Dickens, show time and time again that though death is the last taboo, he thought we ought to try to laugh at it!

I'm glad that the memorial service for Grimaldi featuring a congregation of clowns in full motley is still held each year, and after years of neglect the site of a demolished church in Islington where he is buried is to become a memorial park in his honour. He is one person who would have been delighted at the idea of people walking all over his grave. He'd be even more amused at the fact that the headstone which once adorned his grave now languishes in a shed used by a workman, just like the one he immortalised a century and a half ago!

For Joseph Grimaldi – and I hope for you, the reader – grave moments like these are to be savoured and enjoyed.

Richard De'ath
February 1986

1
GRAVE WORK
Undertakers' Accounts

An Irish undertaker on the scene of a railway accident in County Cork, in 1906, was reported to have told the two assistants who came with him to 'get the dead and the dying into coffins as quickly as possible'.

When one of the men pointed out that some of the victims were alive and might be saved, the man retorted sharply, 'Oh, bedad, if you were to pay any attention to what they say, not one of them would allow that he was dead!'

Retired doctor Omar Philips of Oklahoma was a fastidious man who had carefully arranged every aspect of his life right from his youth. He carried this attention to detail up to the very moment of his death.

For prior to committing suicide with a shotgun in August 1938, he calmly telephoned a local funeral parlour and reported his imminent death – as well as giving instructions for his funeral!

Undertakers have been given some strange instructions in the last wishes of their customers – but few have been more amusing than those made by Tom Bedford of Poole, in Dorset, in 1949.

He asked for his coffin to be stopped on its journey to the cemetery outside his favourite local pub and there left for an hour while his friends had a few drinks at his expense.

'And before the undertaker leaves the pub,' Tom instructed, 'I request that he pours a beer over my coffin, too.'

A Colchester, Essex undertaker found himself with some curious instructions when he was preparing the body of Arthur Smithson for burial, in 1958.

Mr Smithson had for years nursed a fear of being buried alive, and therefore requested that one or more of his toes or fingers be cut off in the mortuary before he was laid in his coffin, 'in order to ensure that I am dead'!

Headline from the *Scarborough Evening Post* of 16 July 1958:

UNDERTAKER'S FAILURE
Let Down By Customers

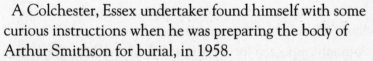

The following report was carried by the *Daily Telegraph* in August 1960:

'Guests at Mr Henry Allen's barbecues in the garden of his house at Milford, New Jersey were upset by the sight of coffins being carried into the adjoining undertaker's premises.

'Mr Allen complained to the town council, which yesterday ordered the undertakers to erect a barrier of trees.'

It was the most embarrassing moment the undertaker in Miami, Florida had ever encountered.

A much respected local citizen had died in May 1966, and a spacious tomb complete with inscribed memorial stone had been ordered and duly erected before the funeral.

It was just moments before the mourners were due to arrive at the cemetery when a horrified assistant pointed out to the firm the terrible mistake that the stonemason had made on the memorial stone.

For in the last name of A. Perfect Whitt the W had become an S . . .

It was more like a scene from the Wild West than a funeral when the cortège of a rich Italian was shattered by a fusillade of shots which peppered one of the finest hearses in Naples, as it carried the man to his last rest in March 1967.

The incident occurred at Casal di Principe, north of

Naples, and was the result of the man's four children deciding to see their father buried in splendour. They approached various undertakers and selected a Neapolitan firm because of its impressive hearse drawn by six black-plumed horses.

All went well until the funeral party was on the way to the cemetery when shots rang out from behind a hedge. At this the coachman in his long black coat and top hat leapt down from the hearse and fled across the fields.

Police regarded the act as being the work of a rival firm of undertakers, jealous at having work taken from them in their territory.

One of the most curious deaths on record must be that of a reclusive and obviously mean undertaker named Osbert James Gardner of Wisconsin, USA who was found frozen to death in bed, in December 1968.

Mr Gardner, who was 91 and had only retired from the family morticians' business the previous year, had ordered the heating to be cut off from his home a few days beforehand because he considered the fuel bill exorbitant.

And yet in a coffin which he had had built years before in preparation for his own death and which he kept beside his bed was found . . . over $200,000 in crisp bank notes!

The bizarre scheme of some German undertakers to recycle coffins came to light during a court case in Dortmund, West Germany, in October 1976.

Before the court were Herr Gerd Fasta and two employees of the Dortmund Municipal Crematorium. Giving evidence against them, Herr Johannes Wassah and his wife.

Said Frau Mathilde Wassah, 'Had it not been for the deaths of two relatives within six months we would never have suspected Herr Fasta, our family undertaker, of being involved in theft.'

To which her husband, Johannes, added, 'Because we were not that close, we bought my Uncle Kurt an oak coffin that had been reduced because of scratching. When we had to cremate his stepsister a few months later we were offered the same coffin, now stained mahogany, as new. But I recognised the scratches.'

The court was told that it had been discovered that by using the lid of one coffin with the base of another, the accused were able to save one complete coffin from every two cremations.

Passing jail sentences, the judge commented, 'The thieves had recycled more than 500 coffins before they were caught. Their procedure yielded enough ash to allay the suspicions of the bereaved.'

After years of working as a mortuary assistant in New

Orleans and never being given an increase in his salary,
Jason Connor began systematically to steal small sums of
money from his employers.

By the autumn of 1977, he had amassed over $2,000
which he kept hidden in his toolbox awaiting the
opportunity to sneak it out of the building.

But when Jason's employers noticed that money was
going missing and instituted a sudden spot-check of the
mortuary, he had to stuff his illgotten gains hastily into one
of the coffins. There he believed it would be safe until after
the search, when he could retrieve it.

Unfortunately, before he could carry out his plan the
coffin went off for cremation . . .

Undertakers have had to accept being the target of jokes
for many generations now.

But in 1977 two irate undertakers in Brighton really
thought the owner of a new shop sandwiched between
their premises had gone too far when she put up her sign.
And so they promptly lodged a formal appeal against her
planning application.

But were their faces red when they learned what the shop
was really going to be used for – a beauty salon. And the
name?

The Body Shop.

A course in 'Death Education' which consisted of visits to graveyards, mortuaries, embalming parlours, as well as lectures by experts such as priests and undertakers, was organised by Mr James Speaker of Ohio, USA, in the spring of 1978.

Hoping to decrease the natural anxiety felt by many people about what he called this 'taboo subject', Mr Speaker also invented a way of measuring established attitudes towards death – on the FOD (Fear of Death) and DA (Death Anxiety) scales.

'Our aim,' he explained, 'was to modify existing reactions to these natural facts. We used a control group to check our results – which were dramatic.

'All our students became more fearful and more anxious as a result of the course,' he said. 'Those measured on the DA scale were less affected than those on the FOD. But we are making progress. Very soon we shall know how to find a consistent Fear and Anxiety Reversal Programme!'

Some years ago, a Surrey mortuary was so busy that a member of the staff with a rather macabre sense of humour posted the following notice on the door:

STANDING ROOM ONLY

The man was promptly dismissed.

The story of 'Speedy' Atkins and his undertaker friend, A. Z. Hamock, became famous all over America in 1980. It happened after 'Speedy' made his first appearance on TV fifty-two years *after* his death!

'Speedy' was a much respected man in his home town of Paducah, Kentucky, who tragically fell into the local river and drowned in 1928. The body was passed into the care of his friend the undertaker, A. Z. Hamock, who out of affection decided to embalm 'Speedy' before laying him to rest in the local cemetery.

By a curious twist of fate, the same river that had drowned 'Speedy' flooded nine years later and brought his coffin back to the surface. In the battered casket, the little man was found 'looking as good as new' to quote his wife, Velma.

Because of this, it was decided 'Speedy' should go on show in the funeral parlour. And when A. Z. died in 1949, the business was taken over by Velma Atkins.

Hearing this story in November 1980, the producers of the nationwide TV show, *That's Incredible*, decided to feature 'Speedy' Atkins.

'When they asked for him to appear on television, I dressed him up in a tuxedo and we got right on the jet,' explained Mrs Atkins.

After making his debut, 'Speedy' became an overnight star – the talk of America. Commented one of the show's organisers, John Caldwell, 'A.Z. did a great job, for "Speedy" looked like he was still alive – apart from the fact that his skin was like wood.

'In fact, he was a lot more lively than some other guests we've had!'

In 1980, an American widow, Mrs Marjorie Toller, announced that she was suing the Plantagenet Casket Company of Michigan for $5 million.

Explaining her case, she said, 'In the middle of my late husband's funeral I suffered a heart attack. The pall-bearers were loading his casket into the hearse when the bottom dropped out and a body that was not my husband's fell on to the road.

'In addition to this strange body, the coffin was stuffed with copies of Playboy magazine, a huge bundle of panty-hose, and about two dozen Coca-Cola cans. Everyone burst out laughing,' she added.

The Grim Reaper was a guest at a party held near Kuala Lumpur, in January 1981. When the supply of spirits ran out, the revellers began drinking a home-made concoction called 'Samu'.

One by one guests collapsed in a stupor, and it was only when the host tried to revive a party-goer and suspected that the man was dead, that it was realised a tragedy had occurred.

And, indeed, before medical assistance could be

summoned, no fewer than twenty-eight of the guests died.

In a later report of the party it was said that all the guests had been . . . undertakers.

Story from the *Eastern Daily Press* of 4 March 1981:

People are being overcharged on funeral costs, the Lord Mayor of Norwich, Mr Ralph Roe, told the city's health committee yesterday.

'Some people are being taken for a ride by funeral directors,' Mr Roe commented.

Mr George Paulos' night out at Castleton House in Dublin, at Christmas 1981, was suddenly interrupted around midnight by a request that someone wanted to speak to him outside. Mr Paulos, an airline manager, who had been looking forward to the evening and had even hired a special dress suit from some Dublin outfitters, went rather reluctantly to the door.

The man waiting to speak to him proved to be an undertaker.

'I am sorry to interrupt your evening,' the sombre figure said, 'but I have a contract with the outfitters and I need that suit you're wearing to dress a corpse that is being buried in the morning at ten o'clock. You see it's the only one the shop has in stock that would fit the dead man!'

The somewhat startled Mr Paulos was told by the undertaker that he had brought a plain suit as a replacement – and still rather dazed the airline manager went off to give up his suit for a dead man!

When Mr Charles Schiller of Boston, USA was made redundant by the firm of undertakers he worked for in 1983, he was given what at first sight seemed an unusual parting gift.

But not so, according to Mr Schiller.

'My leaving present of two elm coffins, with brass fitments, may seem ironic,' he said, 'but this is not the case. I have always wanted to set up on my own, and this is the ideal opportunity. '

An American safety-on-the-roads campaign, in 1983, made use of the image of the hearse to drive home its message.

To combat drunken driving, it was announced that a series of roadside signs were to be erected across the country. The first of these read:

'Drinking drivers, nothing worse
They put the quart before the hearse!'

With the introduction, in 1983, of letters of the alphabet before the numbers on the registration plates of motor vehicles, a London undertaker found the plates on his hearse became grimly appropriate the following year.

Previously, his registration had read 111 URN – but in 1984 when he purchased a new hearse and transferred the old plates, it became B 111 URN.

A pitched battle was fought during a funeral in the black township of Soweto in South Africa, in April 1984, according to a report in the *Rand Daily Mail*.

The paper said that nine people were stabbed in the battle which was caused by rival undertakers clashing. The incident was later blamed on 'business jealousy'.

Two hearse drivers were dismissed by a firm of funeral directors in Cardiff after a number of fiascos, according to a report in *The Times* of September 1984.

These funeral fiascos included a fight between the two men outside the church during a funeral service, and putting topless pin-up pictures in a garage where priests parked.

On another occasion, one of the men went to work in training shoes and white socks, and at a funeral stood in church beside a coffin combing his hair. Both men also refused to go out on a call until they had finished their fish and chip lunch.

According to *The Times*, the men dropped their claim for unfair dismissal when an industrial tribunal was told of their record.

Advertisement from the 'Situations Vacant' column of the *Daily Telegraph* of 29 January 1985, placed by a firm of funeral directors in Orpington, Kent:

DUE TO BEREAVEMENTS we have vacancies for funeral directors. For further details of our salaries, free medical insurance, and death in service benefit, please contact . . .

According to a report in *Paris Match*, in March 1985, there have been some unseemly scenes in the French capital in recent months with rival hearses battling for possession of bodies. This has resulted from a declaration that a 1904 bill which gave local authorities exclusive undertaking rights was illegal.

'In the latest incident earlier this month,' the paper reported, 'the Gaullist mayor of a Paris suburb prevented the porters of an undertaker with anti-Gaullist sympathies from carrying a coffin into a church in his district. The mourners had to bury the body themselves.'

Three masked gunmen made a grave mistake when they decided to rob a crematorium in Enfield, Middlesex, in April 1985.

The men burst into the Enfield Crematorium and tied up the twenty members of staff while they waited for a security van to deliver the wages.

But the bungling bandits didn't know that the security firm had switched their delivery time until six hours later – and after a frustrating wait of an hour the men went off empty-handed.

'Their big plans were left in ashes,' a police spokesman said later.

An undertaker bought forty-four coffins which had been stolen from a rival for the bargain price of £10 each, according to a report in *The Times* of 19 April 1985.

Appearing before Marylebone Magistrates Court, James Shackleton was said to have told the police he knew the coffins were stolen, but the price was 'too good to pass up'.

Shackleton told the court the coffins were used for 'low class funerals'.

'There is a lot of rivalry in the funeral business,' the undertaker said, adding that he was out of work because his hearse was damaged and off the road.

Enterprising mortician Danny Morley opened the Family First Casket Outlet, a coffin shop between a discount store and a tanning parlour in a Missouri shopping centre in September 1985, according to a report in the American press.

His prices, he said, were half those charged by funeral contractors and he hoped to turn his burial outfitters into a national chain.

On offer in the Family First Casket Outlet were coffins ranging from a full ceremonial walnut-with-brass model at $1,060 to a cloth-covered cardboard casket at just $50!

'A grave-digger was turned into a public relations officer overnight by Left-wing councillors in Liverpool and told to preach Militant doctrines, it was revealed yesterday' – from the *Daily Mail*, 6 November 1985.

'Dead Right' might be the most apt comment on this report from the *St Albans Observer* of 5 December 1985:

'The mortuary at St Albans City Hospital is an unhealthy place to be, St Albans councillors heard last week.'

Oh, the irony of it!

A report from Jakarta, in January 1986, reported that an Indonesian MP had died in a road accident on his way home after winning a two-day battle in the regional Assembly to secure funds for an item urgently needed by a local city hospital.

The item? A hearse.

The very latest thing in the death business in America is the drive-in funeral parlour, according to a report from *US Today* magazine of January 1986.

The first of these buildings has been opened in Los Angeles (where else?) and a special feature is the see-through plastic coffins which enable relatives to view their deceased without even having to get out of their cars.

There was a shock in store for residents of Morningside in Edinburgh, Scotland, in February 1986, when they awoke one morning to find this sign unfortunately erected outside the premises of the local undertaker:

'Do not attempt to enter box until your exit is clear.'

There have been some singularly appropriate names for undertakers over the years. Take, for example:

DEATH & SONS
of Bildeston, Suffolk

WAKE & PAINE
of Twickenham, Middlesex

Mr BONES
of Glasgow, Scotland

WILL PLANT
of Swansea, Wales

J. POSTHUMUS
of Grand Rapids, Michigan

GOODY P. CREEP
of Salem, Massachusetts

and perhaps the most notable of all:

GROANER DIGGER
of Houston, Texas.

And just a few more suitable names for the record:

In America there are funeral businesses called THE MOLE FUNERAL HOME in Georgia and THE QUICK-PARK FUNERAL PARLOUR in Ohio. Canada has THE WING ON FUNERAL HOME in Toronto, while South Africa has HUMAN & FITT FUNERAL SERVICES in Pretoria.

In Britain, the National Association of Master Masons meet at TOMBLAND in Norwich, Norfolk, while the Secretary of the National Association of Funeral Directors is called RAY HEAVEN.

2
GRAVE EVENTS
Funeral Tales

There are few odder funerals on record than that staged by the Roman poet, Virgil, who spent almost £50,000 burying a *fly*!

The funeral took place at Virgil's town house on the Esquiline Hill in Rome, and was carried out with 'barbaric splendour' to quote one report. There were also funeral orations read by other famous poets, before the fly was laid to rest in Virgil's grounds.

But there was method in the poet's seeming madness. For a decree had been passed in the Second Triumvirate that the lands of the rich could be confiscated to be given as reward to returning war veterans. The only exemption was land in which someone near and dear was buried – and Virgil claimed his immunity on the basis of his pet fly!

Passions were certainly not buried along with the corpse of the famous French poet, Paul Verlaine (1844-96), when his funeral took place in Paris, in January 1896.

No sooner had the graveside service been concluded, than a fierce struggle developed between the poet's publisher and his mistress for possession of the dead man's winding sheet.

And while this disturbance was going on, a light-fingered member of the congregation named Louis Ai stole away with fourteen of the mourners' umbrellas which had been left leaning against a tree while the coffin was lowered into the ground!

Oscar Wilde (1854-1900) delighted in telling the story of the fellow countryman he saw watching a funeral in a rural district of Ireland.

'Is that a funeral?' he enquired of the man.

'Yes, sir, I'm thinking that it is.'

'Is it anybody of distinction?' Wilde added.

'I reckon it is, sir.'

'And who is it that died?'

'The gentleman in the coffin, sir,' came the rustic's reply.

Extract from the 'Vicar's Notes' in the parish magazine of All Saints' Church, Manchester, in 1936:

'I shall be away from the parish attending the Diocesan Clergy School from 21-24 April. It will be convenient if parishioners will abstain from arranging to be buried, or from making other calls on me during this time.'

It was a moment to savour for 88-year-old Mr Wade Millman of Coatsville, Indiana, when he stood up to preach at a funeral service in June 1937 – *his own*!

Over 500 people packed the town's little church – with over 5,000 more outside – to hear Mr Millman declare, 'There never has been such an occasion as this in the world. Columbus wanted to preach his own sermon. So did

Napoleon and Napoleon's wife, but they didn't. I am.'

The service was complete with coffin, pall-bearers and a specially carved tombstone ordered from Switzerland. Mr Millman apologised for delivering his address without a collar or tie, 'but I haven't been able to find one since my wife died'.

He said that he had lived a moderately good life, and had never worried about things, 'because worrying makes you roll over and wear out the bedclothes'.

Mr Millman added that the only thing he was sorry about was that his horse, John, aged 36, was not present in the church to hear his address but he had been frightened away by all the people and traffic outside!

Knowing only too well the old saying, 'You can't take it with you', wealthy Joaquin Felinna, of Vila Boim in Portugal, decided to have the last word on his relatives whom he suspected would squander his hard-earned cash.

And so, in May 1942, as he lay on his death-bed, Joaquin mustered all his strength, gathered together his banknotes in a pile, and ceremonially burned them.

The ashes he then put into an urn – along with a note explaining what he had done and just enough cash to pay for his funeral!

Shortly after the end of the Second World War, Herman Wallischauser and his family who lived in Hechingen, near Stuttgart, were delighted to start receiving food parcels from some relatives in America.

In a country starved of virtually everything, these parcels were a lifeline and always opened with the greatest excitement. In one such delivery, in January 1947, Frau Wallischauser found a tin containing a fine grey powder which she assumed was instant soup.

However, when mixed with water, the soup seemed rather weak, and so the good lady added a little semolina from the same food parcel. Nonetheless, the family ate the dish with relish – declaring it to be the best soup they had ever tasted.

The following morning a letter arrived for the Wallischausers from their relatives in America. It hoped the family would enjoy the latest despatch of food, and added that included with the parcels they would find a small tin.

This, said the letter, contained the ashes of their dead grandmother who had asked for her remains to be returned to Germany for scattering on her native soil . . .

At the funeral of the famous Hollywood film star, Humphrey Bogart, in 1957, his widow, Lauren Bacall, surprised mourners by having a whistle placed in the urn containing his ashes.

Explained Miss Bacall later, 'It's because of what I said to

him in the first film we made together, *To Have and Have Not* (1943) – If you need anything, just whistle!'

The funeral of Anna Bochinsky was going according to plan in the village of Moinesti in Romania, in the spring of 1959. The coffin, with its lid open as is customary in the country, was just about to be lowered into the ground, when suddenly the 'corpse' sat bolt upright.

The mourners stood rooted to the spot in dumb astonishment as the woman then jumped from her coffin and without a word ran quickly away.

They were even more horrified when Anna ran out of the cemetery, across the road, and was killed by a passing motor car.

There is a story told in Newcastle about an old woman who was standing outside a Bingo hall waiting for it to open, when a funeral procession suddenly went by.

At this, the old lady broke away from the queue, crossed the road to the hearse, and carefully placed a red rose on the coffin.

When she rejoined the queue, there were several kind remarks passed by those standing alongside her.

'My, what a beautiful thing to do,' said one.

'Eee, not many folks would do that these days,' said another.

And a third added, 'That was a lovely thought, hinney.'

'Oh, well,' said the woman after a moment's pause, 'it was the least I could do for him – he was a good husband to me.'

A lucky escape turned into a fatal mistake for Arthur McAlisdair while he was watching a funeral procession in San Diego, California, in May 1960. For in order to get a better view of the proceedings, he tried to run across the road in front of the hearse and was knocked over.

Though he was not hurt, Arthur was immediately urged by an onlooker to lie still and feign injury so that he could claim compensation.

Unfortunately, as he did so, the driver of the hearse leapt from his vehicle to see that his victim was all right – leaving his handbrake off in his haste – and the big vehicle rolled forward, crushing Arthur to death.

At the close of a funeral in Cape Town, South Africa, in June 1965, a mourner was just about to leave the graveside when she realised that her small floral hat had fallen from her head.

Anxiously, the woman looked around the spot where she had been standing, for she planned to wear the hat to a

cocktail party later in the day. But there was no sign of it.

Later, a shamefaced undertaker confessed he had mistaken the hat for a floral tribute and buried it with the coffin!

Aware that he was dying of lung cancer, retired university teacher, Dr James Beckford of Glendale, California, decided to have his body frozen in liquid nitrogen so that it might be restored when a cure for the dreaded disease had been found.

After the doctor's death, aged 73, in January 1967, three members of the Cryonics Society lead by Dr Dante Brunel carried out his wishes by freezing the body prior to its being transported to Phoenix, Arizona, for storing.

Explained Mr Raymond Vest of the Cryonics Society, 'It took eight hours to freeze the body. The doctor's widow was present, as was his son, Norman. We had to send Norman out for more ice once.'

In order to prepare herself for mourning at the funeral of her father, a former snake charmer who lived in New Delhi, India, 23-year-old Suva Mohotti spent the night before the ceremony carefully washing her long hair and piling it up into a bun on her head.

But as she stood by the graveside the next day, she

suddenly collapsed and died. A doctor who inspected
Suva's body found a bite mark on her neck and diagnosed
that a small poisonous snake must have coiled up in her
bun during the night.

Returning to his home in Latheron after a research trip in
the mountains of eastern Scotland, botanist Mr Fergus
Wick was confronted by the sight of a coffin being brought
out of the house and placed in a hearse.

Horrified that either his wife or daughter had died during
his absence, Mr Wick rushed up to the group of mourners.
After a moment's stunned silence, he was greeted by
hysterical shrieks.

The mourners – who included his wife and daughter -
were convinced that it was *he* who was dead and lying in
the coffin!

It was later explained that a body had been found floating
in a nearby lake and had been identified by both Mrs Wick
and her daughter – as well as two family friends and the
local dentist – as that of Mr Wick.

After he had inspected the body in the coffin, Fergus
Wick said, 'It doesn't look anything like me – but I am glad
to be alive!'

A practical joker in California named Martin Olsen

conspired with two of his friends in 1971 to make the day of his funeral – when it eventually arrived – an explosive one.

He made arrangements that after his death, his body was to be taken to a Los Angeles mortuary and there placed in a coffin stuffed with fireworks.

Explained Martin, 'I want to go out with a big bang when they cremate me.'

Printed in the order of service for the funeral of Mr Daniel Patrick Murphy of Brooklyn, New York, in February 1971, were the following words:

'To relieve the monotony of sitting, while the coffin is removed for transportation to the cemetery, mourners are asked to rise during the singing of the chorus, "Fix'd in His everlasting seat".'

Actor and writer Jeremy Lloyd revealed in 1973 that he was leaving the most unusual instructions for his funeral.

'I am always very depressed by graveyards,' he told the *Sunday Express* in October of that year. 'So whatever is left in my bank account I want used to buy a hillside with a cave in it and, wearing my velvet jacket, I want to be put sitting on a chair gazing out of the entrance.

'I think there are one or two fairly cheap caves in the Highlands,' he added.

It was no ordinary funeral when they buried Ferdnand Bachelard, the 'Biggest Man in the World', at Rocourt, a Belgian village near the border with France, on 6 January 1976.

Aged 53, 7ft 9ins tall and weighing a massive 42 stone, Ferdnand died from heart failure during an operation, after years of performing in circuses all over the globe as 'The Atlas Giant'.

It took twelve bearers to carry his huge coffin from the village church to the cemetery. His giant's grave had taken two grave-diggers three days to complete, and filling it in required another twelve hours' work.

His tombstone, though, was just 12 inches tall!

It was the kind of interruption to startle anyone. But as the priest was saying the final prayers over the open grave of 52-year-old Picu Aymaran, at Chaobomba in Bolivia, the lid of the coffin was thrown back and the good lady scrambled out!

Although Picu had been confirmed dead by two doctors before the funeral, she was clearly still alive – and had a bizarre story to tell her amazed relatives.

'I was in Heaven and saw the Glory of the Lord,' she claimed. 'It was perfect bliss, the colours were indescribably brilliant. I had a feeling of weightlessness.

'Then all of a sudden a voice told me to go back to Earth,' she added.

Sixty-six-year-old Henry Taylor was one of four pall-bearers at a funeral in Kensal Green Cemetery in London, in 1977. The coffin the men were carrying was known to be lined with lead and consequently required particular care as it was manoeuvred down a narrow path to the grave.

Just as the quartet neared the grave, however, the four men were required to execute a neat reverse of half a dozen steps. Though well used to such turns, Henry Taylor unfortunately stumbled and fell.

Unable to hang on to the heavy coffin without support at all its corners, the other three men let go . . . and it fell on to Henry, fatally injuring him.

After the funeral service for a close friend in January 1978, two men in Thonburi, Thailand began to argue about the mysteries of life and death. When they then started to dispute the problem of the chicken and the egg

and which came first, the argument turned to blows and one man tragically killed the other.

The dead man had maintained it was the egg.

After conducting a funeral service for a well-known local drunkard, Arthur Mage, in December 1978, the Revd James Owen of Cambridge received a number of complaints from parishioners.

'One is never surprised at the lack of charity that exists,' he said of the service which was attended by members of the police force, the local Publicans' Association and Alcoholics Anonymous.

A memorial address was also given by Dr Michael Avon who said, 'Arthur was born to suffer. Often he was mugged for the money it had taken him days to beg.

'It is true that he was a homeless alcoholic who made well over a hundred appearances before the bench,' added Dr Avon. 'However, he once gave me the most perfect definition of the Christian life . . . unfortunately it was some years ago and I have lost the piece of paper on which I jotted it down.'

There was a surprise in store for Mrs Christine Jay when she arrived for a funeral at Studland near Swanage in Dorset, in June 1979. For she had travelled all the way from her home in Montreal, Canada with her husband, for the funeral of her grandmother – only to find the old lady was still alive.

'We were quite surprised to find Granny Dade up and about,' said Mrs Jay.

The old lady herself explained what had happened.

'Most people only meet at funerals nowadays,' said Granny Dade. 'Therefore I decided to have my "end-of-term" party while I was still active. In the end so many people turned up we had to hire the village hall!'

There are lots of stories of bizarre instructions left by people about the disposal of their ashes. Tony Gribble of Bristol, for instance, said that he wanted his remains to be used as the family's egg-timer 'so that I shall continue to be of use after death', while horse-racing enthusiast Jack Greenslade of Berkshire asked for his ashes to be scattered on the winning line at Ascot where he had not missed a meeting in forty years, 'so that I can watch the winners go by'.

Then there was Ted Haynes, the landlord of the Harbour Tavern in Newhaven, Sussex, who asked for the urn containing his ashes to be placed behind the bar; while an old American submariner, Hiram Cassidy of Louisiana, asked for his remains to rest in the deep – shot from the torpedo tube of his boat, the *Barracuda*.

But perhaps the most amusing story of all concerns wealthy oil lamp manufacturer, Sydney Sherwood, who prided himself on the tidiness of his works in Birmingham. His instructions were that his ashes were to be scattered over the workshop floor, 'because of my affection for the place'.

They didn't remain there for long, though – because just as in life, the place was neatly swept up again shortly afterwards!

On the morning of 28 July 1980, a number of family relatives gathered in the home of Mrs Joan Carson of Lake Kushaugua in New York State. They had come to pay their last respects to the lady who had been certified dead from heart disease.

As they gazed at the open coffin, however, Mrs Carson suddenly sat up and gazed wonderingly about her.

And at this, her daughter dropped dead from fright.

A funeral service which it had been hoped would help reconcile two branches of the Methodist Church in Africa went somewhat wrong in August 1981.

As Mr J. J. Matote, the Member of Parliament for Cofimvoba, in the Transkei, was reading a funeral oration for his friend, Mr H. Gwenshe, he suddenly produced a pistol from his pocket.

Mourners looked on in some alarm as Mr Matote continued, 'I will fire this in honour of my dead friend.'

He then pulled the trigger and shot the officiating clergyman, the Revd V. Nyobole, in the leg.

At this, the service ended in disarray and Mr Matote was charged with attempted murder.

The strangest funeral on record took place in October 1982 in the United Arab Emirates, according to a report in the *Khaleej Times*.

Over fifty mourners attended the service which was accompanied by prayer and songs. The chief mourner was also the person most directly involved with the bereavement.

For the ceremony was to mark the 'death' of one of the man's legs severed in an accident – prior to its burial in a specially built tomb!

The bad luck associated with the number thirteen came true yet again in China, in 1983.

On the morning of Friday 13 May, a group of 13 people were struck and killed by a number 13 train while crossing a railway track in District 13 of Peking.

They were all members of the same family, too – and on their way to a funeral!

The American playwright Tennessee Williams (1912-83) lived a controversial and often bizarre life. But the strangest event of all he reserved until his death.

In his will, Williams asked to be cremated and then have his ashes scattered in the Gulf of Mexico at the exact spot where his favourite poet, Hart Crane, committed suicide by jumping from a ferry.

Williams explained his request in these words, 'I never met Crane – but this will be my chance!'

The funeral procession for the famous screen Tarzan, Johnny Weissmuller, in Acapulco in January 1984, was staged in typical Hollywood style and attended by several thousand fans.

'We arranged for an ape to lead the procession, walking beside the coffin and with his hand upon it,' explained one of the organisers, Mrs June Views. 'Then, as Johnny was laid to rest, twenty loud-speakers rang out with his famous jungle-cry!'

It was a funeral the like of which the dour Yorkshire town of Bradford had never seen before. It happened on 26 January 1984, when 62-year-old Billy Ellison, known locally as 'Chief Lame Fox' and 'The Best Indian in Town' was given a Sioux funeral!

Billy's coffin was draped with a bearskin and decorated with a traditional Indian head-dress and pipes of peace.

Several of the mourners were actually dressed as Indians – and a ceremonial dance finally saw the old chief off to the happy hunting grounds in the sky.

Relatives who had paid to have the ashes of their dear departed scattered from a plane over the Pacific Ocean or on the peaks of the Sierra Nevada mountains, were distressed to discover in June 1984 that they had actually been dumped in a field outside San Francisco.

The relatives who first uncovered the fraud planned to sue the pilot for emotional damage. But theirs was nothing like the problem faced by the local police.

For reports indicated that the dump of ashes, representing as many as 9,000 people, was up to a foot deep. And the police were unsure as to whether they could charge the pilot under a law which forbids 'the co-mingling of human remains'.

Taxidermist Neil Dewhurst of Bridgnorth, Shropshire, who has worked on everything from alligators to a two-headed lamb, was amazed when a caller in September 1984 asked him, 'Please stuff my grandad.'

The woman told Neil that she and her family did not

want to bury their much loved old grandfather – but have him stuffed and dressed in his military uniform to stand in the hall!

'The enquiry was unbelievable,' said Neil later, 'but I'm sure the woman meant it. I had to refuse, though, because I thought it might be illegal.'

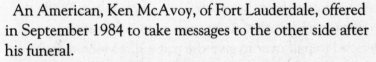

An American, Ken McAvoy, of Fort Lauderdale, offered in September 1984 to take messages to the other side after his funeral.

Expecting to die within four months because of a brain tumour, McAvoy advertised in a south Florida magazine to deliver messages from the living to their departed relatives at $50 a time.

Said McAvoy, 'My mission, when I make the transition into the other world, is to help others. Upon my death, I will be brain dead, then cremated, and the message goes with me. That's the best way I can explain it.

'Take my word for it,' he added, 'I'm guaranteeing I'll find people whether there are 25 or 2,500. I *will* follow through.'

A vast, palatial mausoleum was erected in Jammu, the winter capital of Kashmir, in November 1984, as a memorial to a victim of Sikh extremists.

The killing had touched off widespread protests and the mausoleum was erected by militant Hindus.

It contained only the head of the victim . . . a cow.

A funny thing happened to a London merchant banker, Mark Murphy, on his way to a funeral along the M4 in June 1985.

As he drove along, he spotted two hitch-hikers beside the motorway and, with time to spare before the service, decided to pull over to give the pair a lift. Much to his surprise, Mark discovered the two men were comedian Billy Connolly and singer Rod Stewart.

The entertainers told Murphy that they had been forced to thumb a lift after Rod Stewart lent his Mercedes to members of his family, like him en route for Heathrow, whose van had broken down.

Mark was so amazed that he asked for the pair's autographs 'in case the other funeral guests thought I had been hallucinating', he said later.

And his reward for this kindness? Minutes later, Mark Murphy was stopped by the police for driving – in great confusion – on the motorway's hard shoulder!

The deepest memorial service on record must surely be that for Dr Oliver Lloyd which was held 500 feet

underground at Swildon's Hole, near Priddy, Somerset, in August 1985.

Several dozen friends gathered in the subterranean vault to honour pathologist Dr Lloyd, who had died the previous year aged 73. While alive, he had regularly held birthday parties in the same place!

The winning letter in a 'Laugh – I Could Have Died!' competition organised by the *Sunday Mirror*, in October 1985, for readers' most embarrassing moments was this entry from Mrs R. Stanton of Chester:

'Jumping off a train I saw several members of a family about to get on. "Oh! " I enthused, "a happy family gathering. How lovely."

' "Actually," came the reply, "we're just going to bury my mother." '

The ultimate prize was announced for anyone scoring a hole-in-one at the eighth hole in the New South Wales PGA Tournament, in Australia, in November 1985. The sum of $10,000 in cash or . . . a lavish funeral complete with ornamental tombstone.

If a play-off was needed to decide the winner, the organisers added, the eighth hole would – appropriately – be used as the sudden death hole!

Things went fatally wrong for a group of French mourners keeping a midnight vigil around the coffin of a 97-year-old neighbour who had died on 12 December 1985 at Villeparisis, to the south-east of Paris.

The mourners, all in their eighties, were found dead alongside the coffin the following morning – they were asphyxiated by the fumes of a defective gas heater put on to keep them warm.

It was only at his funeral that eccentric Eric Camp got what he had wanted for most of his life – to be treated as a woman.

For when 82-year-old Eric was buried in January 1986, he was dressed as a woman in his coffin, and during the funeral service at Baldock, Hertfordshire, he was also referred to by the vicar as 'she'.

It was not until he was 77 that Eric decided to become a woman – but doctors then told him he was too old for a sex change operation. So the six-foot pensioner lived the last years of his life as 'Marion' wearing make-up and dresses.

His coffin also bore the inscription, 'Marion'.

Eccentric farmer Vasser Rowe of Clavering in Essex hated funerals – especially slow-moving cortèges. So he demanded a speedy, stylish send-off when his time came,

and that was exactly what his life-long friend the local undertaker, Alan Peasgood, gave him in January 1986.

For during the six-mile journey from Clavering to the chapel of rest in Saffron Walden, Mr Peasgood put his foot down in his hearse and at one point reached the far from funereal speed of sixty-seven miles per hour!

'I'm just sorry I didn't make it to seventy,' Mr Peasgood said afterwards. 'But I'm sure Vasser would have approved. He was a great character and not a man to dawdle. And it was seven miles above the speed limit for the winding country roads!'

Mrs Evangeline Riterman of Chicago, USA became so angry listening to a preacher conducting the funeral service of a distinguished local citizen on her television, in February 1986, that she picked up the set in her sixth floor apartment and hurled it to the floor where it exploded.

That was the unhappy lady's explanation when she was later charged with manslaughter because of a death caused by the fire which followed.

The Americans have come up with a bizarre new form of burial, it was announced recently in *The Mortician's Journal*.

The aim is to reduce the body mass without cremation. First, the corpse is cooled by liquid nitrogen to minus 100

degrees Centigrade, which makes all the body tissue rock solid. Then the frozen body is pulverised by an automatic hammer until all the chunks of bone, head, etc. do not exceed half an inch in size.

Lastly, the particles are reduced to 5 per cent of their original weight by 'freeze drying', which takes out all body fluids.

What is left, the Journal adds, 'can be stored in an urn for burial or domestic storage'.

It will be the ultimate funeral – your ashes despatched into space in a tiny gold-coloured capsule that will remain suspended 1,900 miles above the Earth for 63 million years.

For an estimated cost of $3,900 per capsule, The Celestis Group of Florida, USA plans to launch the first such 'last resting place in orbit' in 1987.

Talking about the plans for these 'space mausoleums' in 1985, a spokesman said, 'With this method, the remains will never be disturbed again – it's not like having to put up with a road going through a cemetery.

'Future mourners will be able to send the sacred remains of their loved ones into undisturbed rest in the sterile, eternal and inviolable space with the stars, planets, Moon and Sun as their markers.

'I'm sure it will be seen by many people as an improvement on scattering ashes on their gardens or on a favourite golf course. It destroys the grass, you know,' he added.

3
GRAVE PLACES
Cemetery Stories

In order to prove whether there was life after death or not, naval officer Ben Wangford, an agnostic, requested to be buried in Watford Parish Church with a fig in his hand. If there should be an afterlife, he said, then the fig would germinate in the coffin and burst the tomb.

Several years after his funeral in 1800, the officer's tomb *did* split open and a healthy fig tree appeared.

Body-snatcher Peter Harkan came to an unhappy end in Meath Cemetery, Scotland, in 1823. With two young assistants, he broke into the graveyard one midnight and was just about to remove a corpse when disturbed by a night-watchman.

The two assistants were rather fleeter of foot than Harkan, and had already cleared the cemetery wall when he arrived panting and almost out of breath. Halfway over, his hands were grabbed by the two men. At that same moment, the watchman also arrived and grabbed Harkan's dangling legs.

In the ensuing struggle, both sides pulled so vigorously that the bodysnatcher soon joined the ranks of those he had plundered!

One of the most curious monuments to be erected in a cemetery can be found in the little town of Canden, in Maine, USA.

It is a marble statue some 28 feet high which towers over the tomb of Captain Hanson Gregory who died in 1847.

The statue was raised on the centenary of Captain Gregory's birth to commemorate his great achievement . . . making the hole in the doughnut!

The story of the travelling coffin is one of the most unusual cases of burial on record.

In 1899, the famous actor Charles Francis Coghlan was buried in a cemetery at Galveston, Texas, very close to the shore. On 8 September 1900 a West Indian hurricane swept the Gulf Coast of America, and a torrential flood deluged the Galveston cemetery, uncovering and carrying out to sea a number of coffins including that of Charles Coghlan.

When the hurricane subsided and the tragedy in the cemetery was revealed, no one expected to see any of the coffins again.

But fate had other plans in store. For several months later, after evidently being carried by the Gulf Stream for almost 1,500 miles, the coffin was washed ashore at the appropriately named Fortune Bridge on Prince Edward Island in Canada – the very spot where Coghlan had been born seventy years previously!

Matthew Burnett, a grave-digger in Coventry during the first two decades of this century, was famous for his wit which was in marked contrast to his gloomy appearance.

A much repeated story is told of a mean local businessman who, after Burnett had buried his wife, tried to get him to lower his fee.

For some time the two men haggled, with Burnett quite unwilling to drop his price for a man he knew was well able to afford it. Finally, the grave-digger lost his patience and, glaring at the businessman, pointed in the direction of the grave and shouted:

'Either pay me my due – or up she comes!'

It is said the man paid in some haste!

Not surprisingly, the night before her husband's funeral, Mrs Josephine Anderson of Leadville, in Colorado, found it difficult to sleep.

Despairing of getting any rest, she finally got up, dressed and went for a walk on the night of 30 September 1902.

According to a later report she entered the local cemetery where a grave had already been dug for her husband's coffin. And in the darkness she must have slipped and fallen, for she was found dead at the bottom of the 15-foot shaft the next morning.

The most appropriate name on a tombstone anywhere in the world is to be found in the picturesque Mount Hope Cemetery, at Rochester, near New York. It marks the last resting place of:

WELCOME A. SOULE

Forever in the shadow of death was a certain American miner named J. R. Wilson of Salt Lake City, whose memorial stone erected on his death in 1948 reads:

J. R. WILSON
worked the
GRAVEYARD SHIFT
in the
COFFIN MINE
at the head of
DEAD MAN'S GULCH
near
TOMBSTONE FLAT
in the
FUNERAL RANGE
25 miles from
POISON SPRINGS
in
DEATH VALLEY

Happily, Mr Wilson only died of old age!

An advertisement from the *London Gazette* of 12 November 1946.

> FOR SALE. Gas fire. Hardly used. Simulated flames. A bargain at £10. Contact: Enfield Crematorium.

Even the occupants of graveyards are entitled to a vote in Russia, it seems.

During the infamous rule of Joe Stalin, an election return in 1947 from one of the districts of Moscow gave him more than 100 per cent of the votes!

The count showed that he had achieved 2,122 votes in a constituency of only 1,617 people.

It later transpired that Stalin's over-zealous supporters had added the roll-call of the local cemetery into the total!

Extract from a letter to the *West Sussex County Times* of June 1949:

'I write on behalf of the churchwardens of St Mary's Church to state we think it desirable to make a change in the arrangements for keeping the grass in the cemetery in order, as Mr Brazly is now getting very infirm. We have given him notice to expire at Christmas.'

Antonio Satanassi, the grave-digger of Riofreddo, near Cesena, in southern Italy, was busy digging a new grave on the morning of 17 June 1955, when the earth beneath his feet suddenly crumbled and he fell into the hole. So loose was the soil, that it buried the poor man up to his head.

For some time, Antonio called for help, but according to a local newspaper report, 'No one would come near thinking he was a ghost.'

When, finally, two men did pluck up courage and approach the grave and saw the helpless grave-digger, he had lost consciousness. He was then dug out and taken home, where the first impression was that he must be dead.

At this a priest was called and was in the process of giving Antonio the last rites when – again according to the newspaper – 'the corpse of the grave-digger regained consciousness and scattered all the mourners by his loud imprecations against the excessive superstition of the local population!'

Jim Stanley had thought it might be a bad day from the time he got up on 4 November 1961. First, the alarm had failed to go off to wake him early to get to an important business meeting. Then, a toaster in the family home in Queensland, Australia had caught fire and delayed him further.

The last straw for Jim was when his car failed to start.

Although his wife, June, could not drive he asked her to take the wheel while he gave the vehicle a push.

Starting suddenly, the car took off with Mrs Stanley clinging grimly to the wheel. Despite her lack of skill, she managed to pass over twenty other cars, before careering helplessly into a wall.

Jim Stanley, arriving on the scene shortly afterwards, found his poor wife dead and his car a write-off. The wall she had struck was that of a cemetery.

French businessman Henri Bidard became famous in 1963 for sleeping each night in his garden in a coffin!

Said Henri from his home in Argentan, 'After we die, most of us are destined to spend the rest of eternity inside a coffin. I wanted to get accustomed to being inside one *before* I die.'

Perhaps the weirdest case of coincidence on record was that reported in America, in 1969.

Miles Lucas was driving from New York to his home in New Jersey when his car was suddenly struck by another vehicle. Miles was slammed against the door and fell out on to the road.

His driverless car then continued to weave along the road until it finally crashed through a wall and came to a stop just beyond.

The wall was, in fact, that of a cemetery, and when the uninjured Miles Lucas arrived to inspect the damage to his car he found it had come to rest against a tombstone bearing the name . . . Miles Lucas!

Statisticians believe the odds against something like that happening are 6,250,000-to-one!

While clearing an area of the Sand Springs Cemetery in Oklahoma, in January 1973, graveyard worker Charlie Hufford discovered what looked like a human hand.

Only *looked* like a human hand, for though it had five fingers, human-like nails and was flesh coloured, there was fur on it and webbing between the fingers.

A local doctor declared it to be . . . a duck's foot!

'The lonely ghost' made a cemetery at Lariano, in central Italy, something of a tourist attraction in December 1973. In fact, the parish priest, Father Don Mantani, found that only a handful of people attended his services, while hundreds congregated outside the cemetery to see the ghost.

According to reports, there was only one ghost in the cemetery because it had only been open a month and contained just one grave – that of Eva Candidi, wife of a local bar keeper.

Scores of people reported seeing a figure in black struggling to get out of the tomb after the cemetery gates were closed at night.

Said cemetery keeper Alberto Galante, 'Some people come from their homes after supper and stand outside the cemetery for hours – sometimes until dawn – hoping to see the ghost.

'The other night when I passed by on my bicycle just before midnight, there were about 1,000 people peering through the railings. I think the ghost is lonely, and until her coffin is joined by others her spirit will seek to escape.'

Topless American dancer, Frenchie Renee, claimed a new world record by being buried alive in a coffin for a month in December 1974 – in company with the four rattlesnakes and a boa constrictor she normally used in her act.

Emerging from her tomb, the exotic dancer from San Francisco drank a glass of champagne and said, 'The burial was the only way I could get a vacation!'

The Society for Perpendicular Interment announced in Melbourne, Australia, in June 1976, a worldwide campaign to have dead people buried upright in cylindrical cardboard coffins.

An official spokesman of the society said in a press statement, 'This is the only way to solve one of our most pressing problems. Horizontal burial just takes up too much room in our overcrowded world.'

A decomposed human arm complete with a hand which was found in a cemetery in Falmouth, Cornwall, in December 1976, had a message attached to it which read: 'In case you need a hand . . .'

It was a curious and recurring dream that disturbed the sleep of Maria Mattei at her home in Rome. For twelve years, in fact, she kept dreaming that she could hear the voice of her dead daughter pleading to be fetched from the coffin in which she had been buried at two years old.

Finally, in May 1977, Maria could bear the dreams no longer and told her parish priest. With his help, permission was obtained to open the tiny coffin and put the distraught housewife's mind at rest.

But on opening the grave, the mystery only deepened. For though the child had obviously been dead all those years, the body looked as if it had only been buried the day before.

You can hear voices from the grave in America – literally. In August 1977, a new gimmick in the burial business was announced in the form of the talking tombstone. When mourners got near enough to the grave it automatically synthesised a message such as:

'Hi, there! I was Jane Smith. I died in 1976 on 16 June at 12.05 pm. Thanks for coming to visit me – and have a good day!'

Explaining how the tombstones worked through a speaker connected to a concealed photoelectric cell, a spokesman of the manufacturers, Creative Tombstones, said: 'With our computerised system people feel their loved ones are still with them.'

As a Mrs Elizabeth Grumpin was praying quietly at the graveside of her sister, Mary, in a New York cemetery in October 1977, the tombstone inexplicably toppled over and trapped her beneath. Though not badly injured, it was still some time before her plaintive cries were heard by other visitors to the cemetery and she was rescued.

Later, during a court case brought against the municipal authorities by the woman's husband, Mr Jim Grumpin, he said, 'It took five hours to get my wife free. I found the incident upsetting because my wife's nephew was crushed to death by a similar gravestone two years ago!'

There were unexpected developments when Mr Maywe
Ndango, a Zambian taxi-driver, picked up Mrs Yona Kikko
in the town of Jerrah, in March 1978.

Tragically, the lady collapsed and died in the taxi – and
though Mr Ndango later sought repayment from the
widower, Mr Brubar Kikko, this was resisted on the grounds
that his charges were above and beyond the agreed fare for
the destination to which Mrs Kikko had been travelling.

Mr Ndango thereupon issued an action against Mr Kikko
explaining, 'The inconvenience of driving to the nearest
cemetery justified the increased fare.'

The military tattoo being put on by the US Army troops
based in West Berlin, in July 1978, was intended to be a
rare spectacle for the thousands of onlookers.

Called 'Patriotism Is Life', the event was highlighted by a
solo parachute jump by Sergeant George McGraw waving a
huge Stars and Stripes flag.

Unfortunately, as the Sergeant fell his parachute lines
became entangled with the flag and he plunged to his
death amidst the tombstones in an adjoining cemetery.

Widow Mrs Beatrice Dingle of Providence, Rhode Island
announced in August 1978 that she was suing the local

Archbishop, Rodney Towler, because for seventeen years she had continuously been praying and leaving flowers at the *wrong* grave.

She explained, 'I thought my husband lay beside Rear Admiral Cloker. But when Mrs Cloker died it was revealed that there was in fact no coffin in the spot adjacent to the Admiral's.

'I have spent thousands of hours on my knees and almost $2,000 on flowers – all at the wrong place. It was wasted time and I blame the Archbishop!'

A little piece of graveyard history was made in Tulsa, USA in February 1980, when a Mrs Skip Switzer asked for her mother to be the first person to be buried in a *pet cemetery*.

She explained, 'We approached the owners of Pawprint Memorial Turf and asked if they would mind mother lying beside "Rinty" her German shepherd dog. They said she could – so we bought the plot and made a miniaturised effigy of mother holding "Rinty's" lead which now stands beside the dog's effigy.

'This makes good family sense,' added Mrs Switzer, 'and we have all decided to share the same resting place when the time comes – each, of course, with our own effigy.'

The occupant of a local cemetery was declared the winner of an election in Texas, in November 1982.

The unhappy loser of the poll was a Republican politician, J. Everett Ware, who was defeated in the election for the South Central Texas District. It was revealed after the count that the winner was Democratic Senator Wilson . . . who had been dead for six weeks!

Alexander Richter of Pennsylvania, USA held a unique record in the annals of burial grounds. For every week for sixty years he placed a wreath on his *own* grave!

As a young man in the twenties, Richter travelled a lot, and after an absence of several years, he returned home to find that the body of a man who had been drowned had been mistaken for him and laid to rest in the family plot reserved for him!

The Chinese couple had just been married – but as the report in the *Peking Daily* of 6 January 1983 put it, 'Death could not part them.' For the pair were both dead and attended the service in their coffins!

Although everything else about the macabre ceremony in Shandong Province was as usual – a priest, lots of guests, piles of presents and a marriage feast – the honeymoon was a return to the graveyard.

The 'ghost marriage' had been arranged by the bride's influential parents after she had been killed in an accident – to prevent her suffering the dishonour of being a spinster in the afterlife.

A matchmaker had been employed by the parents to find a suitable husband – and he came up with an unmarried young man who had died a few weeks earlier.

For the ceremony, both bodies were exhumed – and then afterwards returned together to the husband's tomb while the guests stood by 'eating sweets and burning money and clothing as offerings to the couple', according to the *Peking Daily*.

When London company director Paul Ashton ordered a message in Hebrew to go on his mother's gravestone in July 1984 he did not get quite what he asked for. It was only one word that the stonemason got wrong, but it made all the difference to the sentiments.

It was the rabbi who told a horrified Paul what had happened for instead of the inscription reading, 'She goes happily into the next world', the gravestone read, 'She hiccups into the next world.'

The buxom American singer Dolly Parton confessed in an

interview in July 1984 that she got the inspiration for some of her most haunting melodies while wandering around graveyards!

'They're the one place I can be assured of a bit of peace and quiet,' she was quoted as saying.

The case of the subversive tombstone is unique in cemetery history. For in September 1984, Tan Chu Boon of Singapore was found guilty of erecting a memorial which 'tended to advocate acts prejudicial to the Republic's security'.

The tombstone was placed on the grave of Tan's brother, Chay Wa, who had been executed in Malaysia the previous year for communist underground activities.

The government prosecutor told the court that the inscription glorified Chay Wa by describing him as a revolutionary warrior and a martyr. It also contained other inflammatory terms aimed at overthrowing the governments of Singapore and Malaysia – where communism is outlawed – by violent means, the prosecutor said.

Tan was sentenced to a year in jail (though this was later reduced to a month) and the black marble tombstone officially branded 'a subversive document' – though it still stands to this day!

It was not the kind of sight a graveyard worker usually expected to find in a cemetery – a woman sprawled across a tomb crying, 'Ah, found you at last!'

The bizarre sight occurred in November 1984 at Carisbrooke Cemetery on the Isle of Wight, and the person the worker found apparently talking to the dead was an authoress, Beryl Bainbridge.

Beryl was in fact researching a book about the Revd John Selby Watson who murdered his wife in 1871.

'It had taken me four years to find his grave,' said Beryl, 'but it was so embarrassing. I was just so pleased to find it that I fell on the gravestone without a thought that anyone might be looking!'

To 'celebrate' twenty years in business, the Scunthorpe Municipal Crematorium held an open day in November 1984.

According to reports, three guides took relays of visitors on forty-minute conducted tours against a background of piped music by Richard Clayderman.

Reported one journalist, 'Before the visitors examined the bone crushers and ovens normally heated to 1,000°F, which take seventy-five minutes to burn an average-size corpse, they were given an explanatory leaflet.'

And Mrs Betty Martin, chairman of the council health committee, said, 'People are curious about what happens in a crematorium and we have been able to allay their fears by

showing them. Everyone was delighted by what they saw.'
About 2,000 people attended the open day.

There was an unfortunate choice of words in the
announcement for a contest to find contemporary designs
for cemeteries which was sponsored by the Memorial
Advisory Bureau in February 1985.
Outlining the idea of the contest, the Bureau said that the
main objective was to 'liven up the appearance of
graveyards'!

It was probably the strangest plan ever to come before the
Greater London Council, according to a report in the *Daily
Mirror* of 11 November 1984.
Alternative funerals was the idea – or 'memorial
celebrations' as they were to be called – in cemeteries
reserved for *Women Only*!

If you have a macabre sense of humour (and you surely
must have to have read this book) imagine finding your
final resting place in the cemeteries of any of these little
towns and villages.

In Britain we have: Bubney Moor, Bushy Ruff, Cutty Stubbs, Cool Pilate, Bumper Castle, Thick Withins, Glutton Grange, Butchersick, Dirty Gutter, and Lloyds Nightsafe.

But all pale by comparison with these from America: Midnight (Mississippi), The Boneyard (Arizona), Skull (Nebraska), Skeleton (Oklahoma), Frankenstein (Missouri), Hanging Limb (Tennessee), Bad Axe (Michigan), Cut and Shoot (Houston), Stab (Kentucky), Razor (Texas), Hemlock (Indiana) and – if you can believe it – Transylvania (Virginia) and Bloodsucker Lake in Saskatchewan!

DEATH'S DOOR

This inscription was put on the grave of William Death, a forebear of the author, who died in Wandsworth, London in 1879.

He was not, though, an undertaker, but a . . . stonemason!